Helping Parents With Challenging Children

M000115266

Helping Parents With Challenging Children

M000115266

✓**Programs** *That Work*™

Helping Parents With Challenging Children

Positive Family Intervention

Parent Workbook

V. Mark Durand • Meme Hieneman

OXFORD
UNIVERSITY PRESS

2008

OXFORD

UNIVERSITY PRESS

Oxford University Press, Inc., publishes works that further
Oxford University's objective of excellence
in research, scholarship, and education.

Oxford   New York
Auckland   Cape Town   Dar es Salaam   Hong Kong   Karachi
Kuala Lumpur   Madrid   Melbourne   Mexico City   Nairobi
New Delhi   Shanghai   Taipei   Toronto

With offices in
Argentina   Austria   Brazil   Chile   Czech Republic   France   Greece
Guatemala   Hungary   Italy   Japan   Poland   Portugal   Singapore
South Korea   Switzerland   Thailand   Turkey   Ukraine   Vietnam

Published by Oxford University Press, Inc.
198 Madison Avenue, New York, New York 10016

www.oup.com

Oxford is a registered trademark of Oxford University Press

ISBN 978-0-19-533299-5

About Programs *ThatWork*™

One of the most difficult problems confronting the parents of children with various disorders and diseases is finding the best help available. Everyone is aware of friends or family who have sought treatment from a seemingly reputable practitioner, only to find out later from another doctor that the original diagnosis was wrong or the treatments recommended were inappropriate or perhaps even harmful. Most parents or family members address this problem by reading everything they can about their children's symptoms, seeking out information on the Internet, or aggressively asking around to tap knowledge from friends and acquaintances. Governments and health care policymakers are also aware that people in need don't always get the best treatments—something they refer to as "variability in health care practices."

Now health care systems around the world are attempting to correct this variability by introducing "evidence-based practice." This simply means that it is in everyone's interest that patients of all ages get the most up-to-date and effective care for a particular problem. Health care policymakers have also recognized that it is very useful to give consumers of health care as much information as possible, so that they can make intelligent decisions in a collaborative effort to improve health and mental health. This series, Programs *ThatWork*™, is designed to accomplish just that for children suffering from behavioral health problems. Only the latest and most effective interventions for particular problems are described in user-friendly language. To be included in this series, each treatment program must pass the highest standards of evidence available, as determined by a scientific advisory board. Thus, when parents with children suffering from these problems or their family members seek out an expert clinician who is familiar with these interventions and decide that they are appropriate, they will have confidence that they are receiving the best care available. Of course, only your health care professional can decide on the right mix of treatments for your child.

This workbook is designed to help you address your child's behavior problems and take a more positive approach to your child. It outlines a program to better the lives of your child and your family. You will learn strategies to improve your child's behavior, as well as how to be more optimistic in your thinking. Each chapter provides assessment tools and forms to track your child's progress. This program is most effectively applied by working in collaboration with your clinician.

David H. Barlow, Editor-in-Chief
Programs *That Work*™
Boston, Massachusetts

Contents

Overview

Introduction to Training

The purpose of these sessions is to teach you how to understand and address your child's problem behavior. With the help of your facilitator, you will be learning about the things that affect your child's behavior and creating a behavior support plan that works for your child and family. Your facilitator also will be getting to know you and how you think about your child's behavior. Throughout the training, you will be using this workbook for homework and self-study.

Positive Behavior Support

The particular set of approaches used in this program is commonly referred to as positive behavior support—or PBS for short. PBS is a research-based approach that has been shown to be very effective with a range of persons and behavior problems. PBS helps parents and others understand what causes children's behavior so they can select the right strategies to improve it.

Key features of PBS and this program include assessments that help to find out why a child is misbehaving and steps to improve behavior. Parents team up with facilitators and others who support their children to design a behavior support plan. The overall goal is not only to change a child's behavior but to improve family life in general. Your facilitator will guide you through the PBS process, including all of the following areas.

Assessment

Parents and facilitators need to know why a child is misbehaving in order to design a successful plan. First, they look at the situations that seem to set the stage or provoke behavior problems. They also look at what the child may be gaining or avoiding by misbehaving. By understanding the purpose of problem behaviors and what seems to set off these behaviors, they are then able to develop effective solutions.

Prevention

Knowing the situations that provoke behavior problems can help in crafting short-term prevention strategies. Prevention strategies can include:

- Avoiding particularly difficult circumstances (e.g., seating a child away from a disruptive peer)

- Changing aspects of activities to make them more pleasurable (e.g., allowing a child to listen to music while waiting)

- Providing reminders for a child to use expected behavior (e.g., using visual cues to put toys away)

Temporarily making changes in certain types of circumstances can often remove the trigger for behavior problems, making them less likely to occur.

Teaching

Long-term change in difficult behaviors requires teaching children new skills. This program focuses on helping children learn strategies to deal with challenging situations. Children may also need help developing better ways to get their needs and wants met. Depending on the situation, this may involve teaching a child skills for better communicating his needs, interacting with other people, dealing with stressful or unpleasant circumstances, or becoming more independent in daily tasks.

Management

This program will emphasize how the results of a child's behavior, including the way in which people react to it, can determine whether the behavior will continue. It is important that parents do not unintentionally encourage the problem. The goals are to respond in ways that strengthen positive behavior and discourage outcomes that reward misbehavior. For example, providing attention only when the child is actively engaged in a task reinforces this type of positive behavior. Not allowing the child to leave an unpleasant situation when he acts inappropriately keeps the child from misbehaving in order to escape. Note that because PBS emphasizes a positive approach, efforts to punish behavior are discouraged.

Changing Lives

Sometimes it is important to consider the "bigger picture" when looking at making changes that improve behavior. This program takes the child's overall well-being into account. The intervention process aims to improve general life satisfaction. This may include creating friendships or re-assessing educational goals and home expectations. The PBS process encourages parents to step back from the day-to-day crises to reconsider what's truly important to their families.

Collaboration

Success in changing significant child behavior problems requires input and support from a variety of important people: parents, other family members, teachers, therapists, friends, and anyone else who could have an impact on what happens with a child's behavior. This type of working relationship requires that everyone communicate openly with one another and develop plans that make sense everywhere problems occur. This collaboration is essential for understanding a child's behavior, putting strategies in place, and making sure they work.

Importance of Thoughts and Feelings

An important part of this program is examining your self-talk, or the things you say to yourself when dealing with your child's behavior. During each week you will be recording your thoughts and feelings about your child's behavior and your efforts as a parent. You will learn ways to stop negative thinking and change your thoughts for the better. This process can help you become more productive and confident when approaching your child's behavior.

Use of this Workbook

Your active participation is essential to this program. During each session, you will be working with your facilitator to practice optimistic thinking and address your child's behavior. It is up to you to carry out the assessment and intervention strategies with your child. This workbook includes all of the materials you will need to participate in the sessions. Each chapter corresponds to a session and includes goals and a review of the content covered in session. This workbook also includes instructions and forms to help you design a behavior support plan and put it into effect. Some of these exercises will be started in session, so it is important that you bring your workbook to every session. Your facilitator will also be reviewing your homework each week to check on your progress.

To get the most out of the program, follow these suggestions. First, come to all of the sessions. If you need to reschedule, let your facilitator know. Second, let your facilitator know if you do not understand something or want additional examples. Some of the ideas you will learn may be pretty new or complicated, but your facilitator can help you feel comfortable with them. Third, try to complete the homework each week. It is important to keep up, as the sessions are designed to build upon one another. The more prepared you are for each session, the more you will get out of the program.

Session 1   *Introduction and Goal Setting*

Goals

- To understand the importance of thoughts and feelings

- To learn about positive behavior support (PBS)

- To determine who needs to be involved

- To establish goals for your child and family

- To define behaviors of concern

- To begin keeping track of behavior

Thoughts and Feelings

As you develop a plan for your child, your facilitator will also ask you to share your thoughts and feelings about your child's behavior. There are a couple of reasons for this. First, this will help your facilitator get to know you and what is important to you. Your facilitator will use this information to help you create a good plan for your child and family. Second, your thoughts can affect your feelings and behavior. Exploring your perceptions may help you to be more successful and better able to overcome any challenges you face.

You will be discussing what you think and feel during each of the sessions, as well as recording your thoughts and feelings between sessions in your Self-Talk Journal. Your facilitator will help you determine what situations prompt positive and negative self-talk. You will begin by listing your child's areas of difficulty and success.

Once you have identified some of your child's difficulties and successes, pick a specific situation (from either area) and record it in the Self-Talk Journal in this chapter. You may photocopy this form as needed (see appendix for an additional copy). Write in the second column what specifically you were feeling and thinking during the situation. Do the same for a situation from the other area (difficulty or success). To clarify your thoughts, ask yourself questions such as: What was I

Self-Talk Journal – Session 1

Situation What happened (success or difficulty)?	Beliefs What did you think or feel (self-talk)?	Comments

thinking when that happened? What exactly does that mean to me? Continue your exploration until you can express your thoughts clearly.

Overview of the PBS Process

The approach to addressing your child's difficult behavior used in these sessions is called positive behavior support, or PBS for short. The background of PBS was introduced in the overview chapter of this workbook, including its key features:

- Assessment

- Prevention

- Teaching

- Management

- Changing Lives

- Collaboration

Review this material as needed, making sure you are comfortable with the goals and features of PBS. Feel free to ask questions of your facilitator to clarify concepts. For more information on PBS, a variety of resources are included in an appendix.

Throughout the sessions, your facilitator will teach you to use PBS to help your child and family. PBS offers a creative, problem-solving process for understanding why a behavior occurs and dealing with it effectively. The process involves five general steps or components focused on improving children's behavior and families' lives. You will proceed through these steps during this program.

Five Steps of PBS

Step 1) Establishing goals: defining the problem, including the child's behaviors of concern and specific changes you want to occur

Step 2) Gathering information: watching the child's behavior and talking to other people to understand why the child is behaving in this manner

Step 3) Analyzing patterns: determining what circumstances are affecting the child's behavior and what the child is getting or avoiding as a result

Step 4) Developing a plan: creating strategies to prevent problems, teaching the child better ways of behaving, and responding appropriately to behaviors when they occur

Step 5) Monitoring results: reviewing progress to ensure that the strategies are working and making changes as needed

Case Study: Ben

The following case study will be used to illustrate the five steps of the PBS process. Examples are interwoven throughout the sessions.

Ben is 3 years old. He is an only child and lives with both of his parents. His father works as a data programmer, and his mother stays at home with him. Ben's grandmother lives nearby and visits the family almost daily. Ben attends a preschool program for children with developmental delays and disabilities from 9:00 to 12:00 on weekdays.

Ben loves to play alone, has a keen interest in animals, and is especially good at working puzzles. Ben has very limited spoken language, using only a few words and more often relying on sounds, gestures, and problem behaviors to get his needs met. Ben has extreme difficulty with changes in activities, routines, or settings. He often refuses attempts by his parents or other children to play with him. When others interrupt his play or change his activity or routine, Ben cries, screams, and drops to the floor. When he is required to go somewhere in the car, he resists getting his shoes on and being taken to the car, and then he continues to cry well into the trip. Ben eats very little at breakfast or lunch and is usually extremely hungry by dinnertime. He then cries and screams until his mother gives him something he wants to eat. He eats his food while wandering around the house. Ben resists tooth brushing and is not potty trained. His parents reluctantly admit that he still sleeps with them every night.

The challenges posed by Ben's disability and problem behavior leave his parents very isolated and discouraged. They feel that they cannot go places or spend time with family and friends. Other than school, they try not to take Ben out. In fact, they take turns running errands, leaving one parent to stay at home with Ben. They cannot leave Ben with babysitters because they feel that nobody else can handle him. Ben's mother believes her husband is denying his disability and is frustrated with her mother-in-law's frequent comments that Ben just needs "proper discipline." All of these things are creating tremendous stress on the marriage and family.

PBS is most effective when everyone who cares for and interacts with a child is involved. This is because, working together, one can be confident that everyone in the child's life agrees on the goals, shares ideas and information openly, understands the patterns associated with the child's behavior, and is committed to follow through with the plan. The PBS process works because everyone is learning together and supporting one another. The people who should be involved in the process include parents, family members, teachers, friends, and others who interact with the child.

Case Example: Ben's Team

To make the PBS process work, both of Ben's parents, his grandmother, and preschool teacher needed to be included. This meant having family meetings and communicating with his teacher through email and conferences.

My Child's Team

Consider who should be involved in the PBS process for your child. At minimum this should include those who know your child best, see your child on a daily basis, and will ultimately be using the plan.

Name: Role:

_____   _____

_____   _____

_____   _____

_____   _____

_____   _____

Once you have decided who should be involved, think about the best way to engage them in the process. Remember that, to work together effectively, everyone must agree to participate, communicate openly and respectfully, and resolve problems together as they arise. This can sometimes be difficult because people often see things quite differently, and these differences can lead to conflict. You may have certain assumptions about the goals, roles, and responsibilities of other people participating in the process. Explore these assumptions in order to collaborate with others more effectively.

Establishing Goals

The first step in the positive behavior support process is to create a clear, positive vision for the future. Before trying to understand and address your child's problem behavior, it is important to consider the broader goals you want to achieve. This program is about more than just changing or stopping behaviors; it is also about making a better life for your child and family.

Broader life goals might focus on:

- Improving your child's health or emotional state

- Making it possible for your child to go more places or do more things

- Giving your child more opportunities to make his own choices

- Enhancing or expanding your child's friendships and other relationships

- Improving family life in general

In establishing these goals, it is important to think about your child's strengths and interests, as well as difficulties. You can then build on your child's strengths, as well as respond to his needs. Identifying goals should be done with your child, family, and other people who care for your child and are involved in his daily life. This will help bring everyone together in working toward a better future, as well as result in greater optimism and motivation to make the necessary changes. Record goals for your child on the Establishing Goals form.

Case Example: Ben's Goals

Ben's family developed the following goals: help him play with other children and adults, better handle transitions and change, and ride in the car and eat with the family without problem behavior. In addition, his parents wanted him to develop more interests (beyond animals and puzzles) and participate in typical childhood experiences, including spending time with friends. They also wanted him to become more independent with his self-care, to sleep alone, and to develop the skills he needed to keep himself safe (e.g., looking out for traffic). Ben's parents wanted to be

Establishing Goals

Consider broad goals for your child and your family. List the most important ones here. Remember to consider your child's strengths and challenges.

1.

2.

3.

4.

5.

able to enjoy life as a family without the constant stress presented by his problem behavior. They hoped to be able to go places and do more things as a family and to reduce the conflict in their lives.

Defining Behaviors of Concern

An important beginning step in trying to understand the patterns surrounding a child's behavior is to define the specific behaviors of concern (those behaviors that are problematic and need to be changed). By defining behavior in this way, parents can:

- Look at the behavior and the possible influences objectively (and gather consistent information)

- Be more consistent when trying to understand and deal with behavior

- Make sure that everyone interacting with a child is addressing the same concerns and is "on the same page"

A child's behavior should be defined in terms of what the child says or does and in ways that are observable and measurable. The description should be specific enough that everyone who is involved in the child's life will immediately know the behavior when it occurs. Defining behavior in this way is often challenging for parents because they have adopted certain beliefs about their children's behavior. These beliefs are evident in the labels parents assign (e.g., impulsive—my child can't control his actions; aggressive—my child is trying to hurt other people). It will be important for you to consider your assumptions and define and observe behavior in ways that limit the impact of these types of beliefs.

Criteria and Examples

Well-defined behavior (that is free of labels or assumptions):

- Describes what the behavior looks like

- Describes what the behavior sounds like

- May include typical examples of the behavior

- Does not use words with unclear meaning

Defining My Child's Behaviors of Concern

Behavior	Definition
1.	
2.	
3.	
4.	
5.	
6.	

The following definition examples for tantrum behavior provide illustrations of clearly and unclearly defined behaviors:

Clear definition: *screaming accompanied by wildly waving arms, kicking legs, lasting for at least one minute*

Unclear definition: *a loud fit that causes everyone to look*

Case Example: Ben's Behaviors of Concern

■ *screaming, crying, and dropping to the floor* ■

Now define your child's most serious behaviors of concern and record the definitions on the My Child's Behaviors of Concern form.

Keeping Track of Behavior

It is often helpful to get an estimate of how often or how long a child's behaviors of concern are happening right from the start of the PBS process. Establishing this "baseline" on how the child behaves before implementing the PBS steps allows parents to evaluate changes after the plan has been put in place. This helps to confirm that what they are doing is effective. Later on, it should become obvious that the child's behavior is improving, and that the plan is working (e.g., because hitting has decreased from about five times per day to about three).

To gather this information about your child's behavior before starting PBS, use the simplest method possible that will show how often, how long, or how difficult your child's behavior is. Some options for recording your child's behavior might include:

1. Counting the behavior (i.e., frequency): making note of every time a child does the behavior

2. Timing the behavior (i.e., duration): recording how long a behavior goes on

3. Rating the seriousness of the behavior (i.e., magnitude): using some kind of scale (e.g., between 1 and 5) to estimate how often the behavior occurred or how bad it was each day

If these methods seem too difficult or time-consuming, you can simply get a sample of behavior. This means limiting your recording to short periods each day. For example, you might just observe what happens prior to going to sleep, rating how bedtime went. See example rows of Ben's behavior on the following forms.

Counting Behaviors

Child: _____   Behavior: _____

Date	Start Time	Stop Time	Tallies	Total
10/13	3:30	4:00	/ / /	3

Timing Behaviors

Child: _____   Behavior: _____

Date	Time Behavior Started	Time Behavior Stopped	Total Time
10/13	3:30	4:00	30 min

Rating Behaviors

Child: _____   Behavior: _____

Rating: 3 = severe   2 = moderate   1 = mild   0 = did not occur

Date	Time/Activity	Behavior Rating	Comments
10/13	3:30–4:00/snack	3 (2) 1 0	Was unable to open snack package and had to ask for help
		3 2 1 0	
		3 2 1 0	
		3 2 1 0	
		3 2 1 0	
		3 2 1 0	
		3 2 1 0	
		3 2 1 0	
		3 2 1 0	
		3 2 1 0	
		3 2 1 0	
		3 2 1 0	
		3 2 1 0	
		3 2 1 0	

Frequency Graph

Child: _____   Behavior: _____

Each day, circle the number of times the behavior occurred. Draw a line from one circled number to the next to create a graph.

10/13	10/14												
10	10	10	10	10	10	10	10	10	10	10	10	10	10
9	9	9	9	9	9	9	9	9	9	9	9	9	9
8	8	8	8	8	8	8	8	8	8	8	8	8	8
7	7	7	7	7	7	7	7	7	7	7	7	7	7
6	6	6	6	6	6	6	6	6	6	6	6	6	6
5	(5)	5	5	5	5	5	5	5	5	5	5	5	5
4	4	4	4	4	4	4	4	4	4	4	4	4	4
(3)	3	3	3	3	3	3	3	3	3	3	3	3	3
2	2	2	2	2	2	2	2	2	2	2	2	2	2
1	1	1	1	1	1	1	1	1	1	1	1	1	1
0	0	0	0	0	0	0	0	0	0	0	0	0	0

Additional blank forms (Counting Behaviors, Timing Behaviors, Rating Behaviors, and Frequency Graph) can be found in an appendix at the back of the book. You may photocopy these forms as needed.

Consider how much time and energy you might be able to put into tracking your child's behavior as well as the pros and cons of each of these forms. Select the strategy that makes the most sense and will be most useful for your child and family. You should also complete a Weekly Progress Report form for tracking changes in your child's behavior each week. A copy of the form is included at the end of each chapter.

Crisis Planning (optional)

If your child is engaging in behavior that is placing himself or others at risk or severely disrupting the environment, discuss with your facilitator ways to ensure safety while developing the behavior support plan. For example, this may involve removing your child from a situation, blocking his behavior (e.g., standing between him and another child), holding him briefly until he calms down, or getting some help. If crisis management strategies are required to manage emergencies, they should be used cautiously (i.e., with the least amount of verbal or physical force to make the child safe) and only long enough for your child to regain control of his own behavior. Everyone who will be intervening in this way should approve of the methods and be capable of using them safely.

Homework

✎ Keep Self-Talk Journal.

✎ Identify the people who will be participating in the PBS process and talk with them to help define the child's behavior and identify goals.

✎ Complete the Defining Behavior form.

✎ Complete the Establishing Goals form.

✎ Complete selected data collection forms (e.g, Counting Behaviors, Timing Behaviors, Rating Behaviors, Frequency Graph).

✎ Complete the Weekly Progress Report.

✎ If needed, develop a crisis plan.

Weekly Progress Report

Child: _____   Parent(s): _____

Our child's behaviors are now happening:

Behavior	Never	A few times	Almost every day	More than once per day	Many times per day	Almost every hour	Many times per hour

Other changes for our child and family: _____

_____

_____

_____

Some new things we tried this week: _____

_____

_____

_____

Session 2   *Gathering Information*

Goals

- To explore the relationship between thoughts and behavior

- To understand the purpose and goals of behavior

- To learn how to gather information through:

  - Observing behavior

  - Interviewing people

  - Recording information

- To begin gathering information

Relationship Between Thoughts and Behavior

Sometimes when parents are feeling overwhelmed and frustrated, they begin thinking negative thoughts. For example, when a child misbehaves, a parent might think "It's all my fault. Things are never going to get better." When parents have these kinds of thoughts, their behavior often changes for the worse. They might give up more easily or do things they know they shouldn't do. Remember, what we think affects what we do.

Consider one of your recent negative beliefs (recorded in the Self-Talk Journal). Can you identify the consequences of that belief—how it affected you and your behavior? How did you react to the situation? Be sure to record your beliefs and their consequences in your Self-Talk Journal. You may photocopy this form as needed (see appendix for an additional copy).

Self-Talk Journal – Session 2

Situation	Beliefs	Consequences	Comments
What happened (success or difficulty)?	What did you think or feel (self-talk)?	What happened as a result (actions)?	
When my son sat down for dinner, he started whining and crying. (difficulty)	I thought "We will never have a normal dinner" and felt tired thinking that meals will always be a problem.	I gave him cookies so he would stop crying.	I know I shouldn't give him cookies before dinner, but I felt that there was no other choice.

Understanding Behavior

To be able to improve your child's behavior, you need to clearly understand the purposes and goals of these behaviors. After priorities have been identified, the next step is to conduct an assessment of what is triggering and maintaining behavior problems. Through this process, you and your facilitator can determine why your child is misbehaving, despite your best efforts. You serve as the eyes and ears of this important process. By collecting information at home, you can give your facilitator an insider's view of what goes on during a typical day and night with your child. You will be using some simple tools to focus on what is going on before your child misbehaves and what happens right after these incidents.

Antecedents

One thing parents need to learn is what tends to precede, or set the stage for, problem behavior, also known as *antecedents*. When trying to determine what triggers or provokes behavior, ask:

- Who is around? (e.g., sister, friends, father, dog, neighbor)

- What are the activities, demands, or expectations? (e.g., playing with toys, cleaning room, getting dressed)

- Where does it occur? (e.g, at home, in the car, at the store, at Grandma's)

- When does it occur? (e.g, in the morning, at dinner, after play dates)

Other events or conditions that do not immediately precede behavior can also affect how a child will behave. These "distant" conditions do not by themselves seem to trigger behavior problems, but they will make these behaviors more likely to occur when the triggers are present. For example, if a child is sick or hungry, she may have trouble behaving in difficult situations. A change in routine or family conflict might also make behavior problems worse. Be sure to identify broader physical or social conditions and events that might affect your child's behavior.

Consequences

Understanding what consequences behaviors produce for a child (for example, getting more attention or getting out of doing something unpleasant) is as important to assessment as knowing what triggers behavior problems. You will need to pay attention to all typical responses and outcomes (consequences) of your child's behavior. This includes formal reactions (e.g., using time-out) as well as informal or unplanned reactions (e.g., saying "stop that," trying to calm the child with soothing words, or simply allowing the child to have her way). The reactions of people who interact with your child on a day-to-day basis may be reinforcing behavior problems through either of the following:

1. what your child gets (i.e., positive reinforcement, such as attention received for misbehaving)

2. what your child avoids (i.e., negative reinforcement such as avoiding unpleasant demands)

Introduction to Information Gathering

The purpose of information gathering is to understand the causes and purposes of children's behavior. There are a number of different ways to find out what is influencing your child's behaviors. Some of these techniques require a great deal of time and need to be supervised closely by behavioral professionals. Fortunately, there are less formal ways of finding out the same information that can be just as effective. They include three general methods: observing behavior, interviewing people, and recording information.

Observing Behavior

Observing, or simply paying attention, is one way of learning more about a child's behavior. The observations of a well-informed parent are invaluable to designing an effective plan. You will need to pay attention to what is happening around your child's behavior, specifically the situations that lead up to the problems and how things change after an incident. The trick is to watch your child with "objective" eyes, not "parent who deals with this child every day" eyes. To focus on your child's behavior objectively, you may need to consider what you are saying to yourself during incidents. The assumptions you are making might be clouding your observations.

Observing means noticing situations in which a child behaves well, in addition to those in which she has difficulty. For each situation, consider who is present, what is happening, and where and when the incident occurs. Remember to pay attention to what your child gets or avoids as a result of the behavior.

Case Example: Observing Ben's Behavior

■ *Ben's parents decided to pay attention to times when Ben could change activities without problems (e.g., when he was going to do something he really liked) and compare them with times that were difficult. They also wanted to look at playtime to try to figure out how involved they could get in Ben's play and how much they could do with him (e.g., sitting near him, handing him toys) before he would resist. They thought that by looking closely at those circumstances they could get a better idea of what was influencing his behavior.* ■

Interviewing People

Another simple and useful method of gathering information about a child's behavior is to "interview" other people. You should talk to the people who know your child well and interact with her in a variety of situations—for example, family members and friends. Also include others who see your child frequently and are familiar with the problem behavior, like teachers and babysitters. Taking the opportunity to discuss concerns and get input from other people allows you to better consider everyone's perceptions and to generate new ideas. It is important to recognize that people might suggest ideas that conflict with your own. You may need to remain open to new perspectives in this process.

During the interviewing process, you should explore:

■ Behavior patterns, considering who, what, where, and when

■ "Distant" events or conditions that might be affecting your child's behavior

■ What happens after: the reactions to or results of the behavior

It is helpful to record what you learn through these discussions, as sometimes it is easier to find a pattern when the information is down on paper. You might want to use the Interview Form provided in this chapter. An additional blank form can be found in an appendix at the back of the book. You may photocopy the form as needed.

Case Example: Interviews about Ben

Note how Ben's parents approached the interviewing process:

■ *Ben's parents decided to make individual lists of the times that things were easy and hard for each of the parents with Ben. They could then compare notes and*

Interview Form

Use the following questions to interview someone who knows your child well. Make sure to ask follow-up questions to help you understand the person's perspective.

1. What do you think are the child's strong points (talents, interests)?

2. What specific behaviors concern you?

3. Under what circumstances are these behaviors most likely?
   - With whom:

   - What activities:

   - Where:

   - When:

4. Under what circumstances are these behaviors least likely?
   - With whom:

   - What activities:

   - Where:

   - When:

5. What does it seem to you that the child is getting or avoiding through these behaviors?

6. Can you think of anything else that might be influencing the child's behavior?

discuss what was happening more objectively, looking at the when, what, and where of their challenges with Ben. They decided to ask the same of Ben's teacher and grandmother. ▪

Recording Information

Recording what is discovered from watching a child is often an essential part of the intervention design process. It can help parents have a more objective view of their children's behavior and circumstances surrounding it. This improves the quality of the assessment and aids in coming up with effective strategies. Your facilitator will help you complete the Motivation Assessment Scale (described next), which can help you to focus on important aspects about why your child might be misbehaving. In addition, you can record on your own, for example by keeping a simple daily journal of the events of the day. You might also want to try more structured methods such as using a Scatterplot form or a Behavior Log to track the details of your child's behavior.

Motivation Assessment Scale

The Motivation Assessment Scale is a screening tool that helps to pinpoint the function, or goal, of a child's problem behavior. It assists in making an educated guess about the motivation for behavior. A child's behavior might be motivated by attention, tangibles (e.g., food, toys), sensory outcomes (e.g., sounds, movement), or escape. It is available for free online at http://www.monacoassociates. com/mas/MAS.html. After completing the MAS, your facilitator will score it for you and discuss the results.

Scatterplot

Parents can record behavior in a way that helps pinpoint the times of day their child's behavior is most and least likely. With this system, parents simply mark whether or not a behavior occurs within a particular period of time. Using this information, parents can narrow down when to look more closely at their child's behavior and the circumstances around it. For example, if Ben's parents were to look at an example that shows the times of day Ben whines, they might want to focus their attention on the early morning, midday, and just prior to dinnertime (see Figure 2.1).

Scatterplot

Child: _____Ben_____   Behavior: _Screaming, crying, and dropping to the floor_

Dates: __5/1__ through ___5/10___

Record the times of day (and/or activities) in which the behavior might occur. Write in the dates for the recording period in the first row. When the behavior occurs, shade in the corresponding box.

Time	Activity	Dates									
		5/1	5/2	5/3	5/4	5/5	5/6	5/7	5/8	5/9	5/10
7–8 a.m.	Preparing for school	▓			▓					▓	
8–9 a.m.	Transition to school		▓							▓	
9–10 a.m.	Arrival/centers				▓						
10–11 a.m.	Outside (transition)			▓							
11–12 p.m.	Swim/change										
12–1 p.m.	Lunch	▓					▓				▓
1–2 p.m.	Transition home				▓			▓			
2–3 p.m.	Arrival home/change										
3–4 p.m.	Home/play alone			▓							
4–5 p.m.	Play outside home										
5–6 p.m.	Dinner		▓		▓		▓			▓	
6–7 p.m.	Bath			▓							
7–8 p.m.	Bedtime										

Figure 2.1

Example of Completed Scatterplot

Source: Adapted from Touchette, P. E., MacDonald, R. F., & Langer, S. N. (1985). A scatterplot for identifying stimulus control of problem behavior. *Journal of Applied Behavior Analysis, 18,* 343–351.

Scatterplot

Child: _____   Behavior: _____

Dates: _____ through _____

Record the times of day (and/or activities) in which the behavior might occur. Write in the dates for the recording period in the first row. When the behavior occurs, shade in the corresponding box.

		Dates									
Time	**Activity**										

Source: Adapted from Touchette, P. E., MacDonald, R. F., & Langer, S. N. (1985). A scatterplot for identifying stimulus control of problem behavior. *Journal of Applied Behavior Analysis, 18,* 343–351.

Behavior Log

Record situations in which your child's behavior is difficult, including specifically what your child says and does and what occurs before and after the behavior.

Antecedent (Before Behavior)	Behavior	Consequence (After Behavior)
Ben's mother asks him to put on his shoes	Ben extends his body, cries, and screams	Ben's mother takes his shoes to the car, letting him go in his bare feet
Ben's mother guides him from the car into school	Ben cries and screams	Classroom assistant hands him a toy and brings him into the class
Ben is told it is time to come inside from the playground	Ben extends his body, cries, screams, and then drops to the ground	Assistant waits for him to get calm and then physically guides him in
Ben's mother sits down to play with him	Ben extends his body, cries, and screams	Ben's mother says "I just want to play with you" and then moves away, leaving him alone
As dinner time nears, Ben's mother goes into the kitchen	Ben walks into the kitchen and begins to cry and then scream	Ben's mother quickly gives him one of his favorite foods
Ben's father asks him to sit at the table to eat	Ben sits briefly and then picks up his food and walks around	Ben's mother asks him to come back or says "don't you want to sit?" and then lets him go

Figure 2.2

Example of Completed Behavior Log for Ben

Behavior Log

Record situations in which your child's behavior is difficult, including specifically what your child says and does and what occurs before and after the behavior.

Antecedent (Before Behavior)	Behavior	Consequence (After Behavior)

A blank copy of a Scatterplot is provided in this chapter. An additional blank form can be found in an appendix at the back of the book. You may photocopy the form as needed.

Behavior Logs

Behavior logs, or ABC charts, are relatively easy to use. When a behavioral problem occurs, parents can record what happened before the incident (the antecedent, or "A"), a description of the behavior itself ("B"), and what happened afterward (the consequence, or "C"). Refer to the example of a behavior log in Figure 2.2.

A blank copy of a Behavior Log is provided in this chapter. An additional blank form can be found in an appendix at the back of the book. You may photocopy the form as needed.

Choosing a Strategy

Choose a strategy that best suits your family's needs and situations. For example, the Behavior Log provides a lot of important information, but it also takes more time to complete than simple checklists (e.g., frequency counts). Using another format such as the Scatterplot first might help you pinpoint the times of the day problem behaviors are most likely and least likely to occur. You can then plan more involved recording just for those times of day. Strategies for keeping a record of your child's behavior should be selected (or designed) based on your family's needs and situations. They should not be ridiculously time-consuming or difficult, or you will find it hard to use them consistently. Furthermore, they should capture the things you and your family are most concerned about. Be realistic about what you can do, even if it simply involves paying attention to a particular situation and talking to a couple of people. Develop a plan for information gathering on the form provided.

Information-Gathering Plan

Observing Behavior:

Interviewing People:

Recording Information:

Homework

✎ Continue to keep Self-Talk Journal.

✎ Continue to complete the Weekly Progress Report.

✎ Develop a plan for gathering information about your child's behavior (e.g., using the Interview Form, Scatterplot, Behavior Log, or some other format if appropriate).

✎ Talk with family members and others to get their input.

✎ Complete the MAS on your child's behavior(s), if it was not completed during the session or if you want to complete additional forms for other behaviors.

Weekly Progress Report

Child: _____ Parent(s): _____

Our child's behaviors are now happening:

Behavior	Never	A few times	Almost every day	More than once per day	Many times per day	Almost every hour	Many times per hour

Other changes for our child and family: _____

_____

_____

Some new things we tried this week: _____

_____

_____

Session 3   *Analysis and Plan Design*

Goals

- To use distraction to deal with unproductive self-talk

- To use information to analyze patterns

- To summarize patterns or generate hypotheses

- To use patterns to brainstorm intervention ideas

Use of Distraction

As you have been keeping track of your thoughts, you may have noticed that negative self-talk has a tendency to keep going and even get worse if left unchecked. You may have to do something to interrupt that way of thinking so that you can handle situations more effectively. At those times, distraction is helpful.

Distraction involves shifting your attention away from any pessimistic thoughts during activities such as dealing with a behavior problem or a stressful workday. This can be done with a variety of methods, for example:

- Singing to oneself

- Choosing a mantra (e.g., "things will soon get better")

- Writing down the belief and throwing the piece of paper away

- Scheduling time to think through the belief (e.g., after work, when the kids are in bed)

- Reading a 3 × 5 note card that says "STOP!"

Consider what distraction strategies you'd like to try and in what situations they might be helpful. Make a note of the strategies you plan to use under the comments section of your Self-Talk Journal. You may photocopy this form as needed (see appendix for an additional copy).

Self-Talk Journal – Session 3

Situation What happened (success or difficulty)?	Beliefs What did you think or feel (self-talk)?	Consequences What happened as a result (actions)?	Comments (e.g., distraction strategies)

In the last couple of sessions, you collected information about your child's behavior. Now you will study the information to figure out patterns affecting your child's behavior. Remember to look for patterns related to what happens before and after the behavior. After collecting information for a week, you might have enough information to come up with first guesses about patterns, but it may take longer to see clear trends. You will need to continue to collect information until the patterns are clear.

The goal is to identify situations that occur again and again, allowing you to predict circumstances in which you are likely to see behavior problems. In other words, you determine what situations are expected to set the stage for behavior and what results or reactions reliably follow behavior. If you already have assumptions about what is affecting your child's behavior, the purpose of this step is to use the collected information to either support or challenge those assumptions.

Review the assessment information, and answer the following questions (see Pattern Analysis Worksheet):

- What are the circumstances (i.e., when, where, with whom, during what activities) in which the behavior is most likely and least likely to happen?

- What are the typical outcomes and reactions (consequences) of the behavior? That is, what does your child get or avoid through his actions?

  Another question that is often helpful to consider is:

- What would cause your child to behave this way, and what would make your child stop?

It is important to recognize that sometimes parents' beliefs about their child or his behavior can have an impact on their expectations. Those expectations, in turn, can have an impact on how parents approach or respond to their child. For example, if a parent thinks "My child can't help behaving this way because he has a disability," the parent will not set high expectations for the child's behavior. When the child does misbehave, the parent might not react in a way that discourages the behavior. If you have such beliefs, these might need to be examined in order to be able to identify patterns objectively.

Keep in mind that some behaviors have more than one purpose or function. For example, children might scream in one situation to get the attention of people around them and scream at another time to express their discomfort with an activity. It is important to identify not only the goals behaviors achieve but also the circumstances in which those functions are meaningful.

Case Example: Ben's Patterns

In the following case example, note the times, places, people, situations, and activities associated with Ben's problem behavior and those in which problems rarely occur. Then consider the consequences that tend to follow the behavior.

- Most likely to misbehave: *sitting at dinner table; transitions to the car, when getting ready to leave the house, or between activities; schedule changes within routines; when his mother or others try to play with him*

- Least likely to misbehave: *playing alone, tickle games, eating meals (while walking around), going swimming (a type of transition), when holding small toys (e.g., stuffed animals)*

- Results: *mother leaves him alone, feeds him quickly, and lets him walk around with food; limits trips in the car; and generally delays transitions*

Broader Issues

As mentioned in Session 2, in addition to the immediate events preceding and following a child's behavior, there might be other conditions or more distant events that are influencing a child's current behavior. These might include:

- Medical conditions (e.g., allergies or dietary problems result in greater irritability, in general)

- Activity patterns (e.g., too many activities lead to resistance when asked to participate in family events)

- Personal relationships (e.g., presence of a friend makes child more willing to participate in activities)

Case Example: Ben's Broader Issues

Note which types of conditions are a problem for Ben in the following case example.

- *In addition to the immediate issues affecting Ben's behavior, there were other concerns. He had a restricted diet and poor sleep patterns, both of which could have been affecting his behavior. Also, because of his problem behavior, he did not have the opportunity to participate in the range of typical activities or have the quality of relationships children his age usually enjoy.* ▦

Creating Hypotheses or Summary Statements

Once parents have identified circumstances that appear to bring about and follow behavior, it is often helpful to summarize these patterns in a phrase, sentence, or short paragraph. The summary can then be used to guide intervention planning. Summary statements should include:

▦ What sets the stage or triggers a child's behavior

▦ What is the behavior of concern (i.e., what the child says or does)

▦ What occurs afterward (what the child gets or avoids as a result)

Case Example: Summary Statements for Ben

For the case example, note the context(s) in which behaviors are a problem, specific behaviors of concern, and the function(s) served by the behavior. Try to also identify any setting events.

▦ *When Ben's parents try to put his shoes on to leave the house, he screams, cries, and drops to the floor. This delays the transition, forces his mother to take him out without shoes, or results in her canceling the errand or getting someone else to do it.*

▦ *When his parents or peers try to play with Ben, he screams and cries; if they don't back off, he turns his back on them or pushes them away. Eventually, the children or family members back off, and Ben is able to continue playing contentedly by himself.*

▦ *When Ben doesn't eat well at breakfast and lunch, he screams and cries as dinnertime approaches. If Mom doesn't feed him right away, he gets louder and runs around the kitchen. As a result, she quickly prepares him something he likes to eat. She often allows Ben to carry his food around (rather than requiring him to sit with the family during meals).*

Testing Hypotheses

At times the patterns are clear, and it is easy to identify what is triggering and maintaining a behavior. However, there are other times when the circumstances surrounding behavior problems are more complex. In this case, it might be helpful to test one's "hypotheses" or best guesses about the purposes of the behavior. Parents do this by setting up situations they think might affect a child's behavior and see what happens (i.e., if the behavior changes). Ultimately, the hypotheses will be confirmed—or not—when the intervention is put into effect. If the strategies work, the parents were right; if they don't, the parents need to investigate further to see if there is anything they missed. See the following example of how to test a hypothesis.

Case Example: Testing Ben's Hypothesis

▨ *To confirm one of Ben's patterns, Ben's mother could alternate requiring and not requiring Ben to wear his shoes and see whether his tantrums predictably occur.* ▨

Pattern Analysis

It is now time to look at all of the information you have collected so far and look for patterns. Use the Pattern Analysis Worksheet to consider the circumstances (when, where, with whom, what activities) and consequences (what your child gets or avoids as a result) of the behavior. If the patterns are not clear, continue to ask yourself probing questions (e.g., "Does that happen every time? If not, why?").

Based on this information, come up with at least one hypothesis or summary statement, including both the contexts and functions of behavior. Record the hypothesis or summary statement on the Pattern Analysis Worksheet provided in this chapter. An additional blank form can be found in an appendix at the back of the book. You may photocopy the form as needed.

You might have difficulty accepting a hypothesis that contradicts your previous assumptions. If this is the case, question your self-talk surrounding that hypothesis.

Using Patterns to Brainstorm Intervention Ideas

You must understand your child's behavior before you can begin to address it effectively. Once you have gathered information and analyzed patterns, you should have a solid understanding of:

▨ The specific behaviors that concern you

▨ The alternative behaviors you would like to teach

Pattern Analysis Worksheet

Behavior(s) of concern (list all behaviors that reliably occur together): _____

_____

_____

Circumstances	Consequences
My child's problem behavior *usually or often* occurs in the following circumstances:	My child's problem behavior *usually or often* results in the following consequences:
When:	My child gets:
Where:	
With whom:	My child avoids:
What activities:	
My child's problem behavior *rarely or infrequently* occurs in the following circumstances:	My child's positive behavior *usually or often* results in the following consequences:
When:	My child gets:
Where:	
With whom:	My child avoids:
What activities:	

Summary Statement:
Write a sentence or short paragraph to describe the patterns in your child's behavior.

- The triggers for your child's best and worst behavior

- The purpose or function of your child's behavior (what your child gets or avoids as a result)

With this information in hand, you and your facilitator can design an effective intervention for your child's behavior. Hopefully, your plans will also improve family life in general.

Identifying Strategies

The behavior support plan is made up of strategies designed so that a child no longer needs problem behavior to achieve his wants and needs. Parents help children learn and use more appropriate behaviors that work better and result in positive outcomes for children (and families!). This might involve changing parents' behavior (including how parents react to their children's behavior) or changing things in the environment that will "set children up" for their best possible behavior. The three general strategies that make up a behavior support plan are:

- **Prevention:** preventing problems by changing circumstances that trigger or set the stage for problem behavior

- **Management:** providing rewarding outcomes for positive behavior and managing consequences to avoid inadvertently rewarding problem behavior

- **Replacement:** teaching children more effective and appropriate ways to communicate their needs and cope with difficult situations

You will use your hypotheses to brainstorm strategies associated with each of these areas.

Brainstorming

Using one of your hypotheses or summary statements, generate ideas for intervention that include preventing problems, managing consequences, and replacing behaviors or teaching skills. Jot these down on the Brainstorming Interventions form provided in this chapter. You will build on these ideas in future sessions (4 through 6). You might want try out the ideas (like with the hypothesis testing) to make sure they work before integrating them into your overall plan. An additional blank Brainstorming Interventions form can be found in an appendix at the back of the book. You may photocopy the form as needed.

Homework

✎ Continue to keep Self-Talk Journal.

✎ Practice using the distraction strategies and record the results in the Self-Talk Journal.

✎ Complete the Weekly Progress Report.

✎ Continue data collection using the method(s) selected in Sessions 1 and 2.

✎ Complete the Pattern Analysis Worksheet.

✎ Complete the Brainstorming Interventions form.

✎ Share summary statements and intervention ideas with family members and others to get their input and agreement.

Brainstorming Interventions

What circumstances set the stage for my child's behavior?	What is my child currently doing that is of concern?	What outcomes does my child achieve through his or her behavior?
		Get:
		Avoid:
PREVENTION:	MANAGEMENT:	REPLACEMENT:
How will I change these things to . . . Avoid difficult situations?	How will I respond to my child's behavior to . . . Reward positive behavior?	What would I like my child to do instead?
Make problem situations better?	Not reward problem behavior?	How will I teach my child to do this?
Add cues to prompt good behavior?		

Weekly Progress Report

Child: _____   Parent(s): _____

Our child's behaviors are now happening:

Behavior	Never	A few times	Almost every day	More than once per day	Many times per day	Almost every hour	Many times per hour

Other changes for our child and family: _____

_____

_____

Some new things we tried this week: _____

_____

_____

Session 4   *Preventing Problems*

Goals

- To understand the disputation process
- To discuss circumstances that increase the likelihood of behavior
- To learn strategies for avoiding difficult situations
- To learn strategies for improving difficult situations
- To learn ways to provide a child with choices
- To learn strategies for prompting good behavior

Disputation Process

In the past few weeks, you have been recording your thoughts and feelings associated with successful and challenging situations for your child. This session introduces a strategy for arguing or challenging unproductive beliefs: the disputation process. The four steps are:

Step 1: Identify the negative belief (i.e., "What exactly do you say to yourself that is pessimistic?").

Step 2: List evidence that supports or refutes the belief (i.e., "What makes you believe that to be true or false?").

Step 3: Find alternative explanations for the problem (i.e., "Are there other possible reasons or motives?").

Step 4: Evaluate the usefulness of maintaining the belief (i.e., "In what ways does that belief benefit you or others or improve the situation?").

Example

Step 1: Identify the negative belief: *Nothing I do makes a difference with my child's behavior.*

Step 2: List evidence that supports or refutes the belief: *My child is still having tantrums every day; however, those tantrums do not go on as long. I also do not have to restrain my child anymore. My actions are making a difference. When I ignore my child's screaming, it initially gets louder and more dramatic, but then it stops.*

Step 3: Find alternative explanations for the problem: *The tantrums are leftovers of the time when I tried to soothe my child rather than withhold attention. Sometimes I still just soothe my child or give her what she wants to make the tantrums stop. This happens particularly when I am feeling inadequate as a parent. I am still trying to teach my child more efficient and effective ways of getting her needs met. Once my child has fully learned these skills, tantrums will not be necessary.*

Step 4: Evaluate the usefulness of maintaining the belief: *When I think "nothing I do makes a difference," I am more likely to give in or respond inconsistently. This actually prolongs or strengthens my child's tantrums.*

Consider one of your recent negative beliefs (recorded in the Self-Talk Journal), and go through the four steps to dispute that belief. Be sure to consider specific details. It might help to ask yourself:

- What exactly happened?

- What was I thinking when that happened?

- How did I react as a result of my thoughts or feelings?

- Do I think the belief is true? If so, why?

- What are other reasons why that could have happened?

- So, given all of this, is this belief helpful?

You may photocopy the Self-Talk Journal form as needed (see appendix for an additional copy).

Self-Talk Journal – Session 4

Situation	Beliefs	Consequences	Disputation	Comments
What happened (success or difficulty)?	What did you think or feel (self-talk)?	What happened as a result (actions)?	Was this a useful or accurate belief?	
When my son sat down for dinner, he started whining and crying. (difficulty)	I thought "I'm a bad mother, and I'm not able to control his behavior."	I gave him cookies so he would stop crying.	Is the belief true? Probably not. Are there other explanations? My son was hungry and tired. Is this belief helpful? No, it just makes me feel bad, and I give up trying.	
			Is the belief true? Are there other explanations? Is this belief helpful?	
			Is the belief true? Are there other explanations? Is this belief helpful?	
			Is the belief true? Are there other explanations? Is this belief helpful?	

Identifying Circumstances that Precede Behavior

As mentioned previously, a range of possible circumstances (referred to as triggers, antecedents, or setting events) can prompt problem behavior. These things can include physical discomfort, stressful situations, withdrawal of attention, demands to do something, changes in routine, and a variety of other issues. They can also include ways in which parents interact with children (e.g., being short-tempered, forgetting to plan ahead). What parents are feeling or thinking during those times can have an impact on such responses.

It is essential that all of these kinds of circumstances—and those that prompt good behavior—be identified. You can use this information to rearrange your child's environment in ways that can prevent problem behaviors from flaring up. When difficult situations arise, ask yourself: What could I change about this situation that would increase the chance that my child would behave better?

Problem behavior may be prevented through a variety of strategies, including avoiding or improving difficult situations, providing choices, or using methods to prompt more positive behavior.

Avoiding Difficult Situations

There are a number of ways behavior problems can be prevented. You have probably already made changes to how you do things to avoid problems. Strategies to avoid difficult situations can be used as temporary measures until you can teach your child alternative behaviors. Here are some possible strategies for avoiding problem circumstances altogether:

1. If a child is disruptive in certain places, during certain activities, or with particular people—and these situations are unnecessary—avoid them (e.g., not shopping when stores are particularly busy, not serving peas).

2. If changing aspects of a child's environment or interrupting a child's routines causes disruption, keep the surroundings or schedule as consistent as possible.

3. If sickness, tiredness, or hunger make a child more likely to misbehave, address those conditions as best as possible, and avoid typical triggers during those times (e.g., not asking the child to do something difficult when she is tired).

4. If a child's problem behavior is thought to be attention-getting, provide a great deal of unconditional attention throughout the day.

5. If a child misbehaves when asked to stop a favorite activity, extend the time available to continue playing or engaging in a preferred activity.

Sometimes avoiding difficult situations is an appropriate and respectful way of responding to a child's needs and interests. However, preventing problems by completely avoiding situations might not always be possible. For example, a child might become upset getting on a school bus, but the child must go to school. Or a child might dislike taking a bath, but she still has to take one. Avoidance could also become a bad habit. Parents might start avoiding more and more situations because they *expect* those situations to be difficult (even if they might not be). Avoidance reduces the range of places, people, and events children experience. Remember it is not natural or helpful for a child to avoid all types of adversity.

Improving Difficult Situations

When it is not practical or possible to avoid a task or situation that causes disruption, parents can still do things to make the experience better for the child. Inserting or embedding pleasant activities can make the whole task or situation more enjoyable. Some examples of successful strategies include:

1. If a child's problem behavior occurs only during particular activities, change the most troublesome parts of those activities to create a more positive experience (e.g., shorten the duration of a task, make the task easier, add favorite music, or include a friend).

2. If a child misbehaves for attention, give her something fun to do (e.g., a toy or a book) while waiting for you or someone else to interact with her again.

3. If interrupting favorite activities causes behavior problems to occur, add a transition activity that is fun or involve the child directly in the steps needed to move to the next activity (e.g., have her turn off the computer or put away a game). Or inform the child of when the next opportunity for the favored activity will be available.

How You Communicate

One important consideration in making difficult situations better is the way in which parents communicate. Not only is what parents say important but also the tone, body language, and kinds of expressions they use. For example, if parents approach a child expecting resistance, it might show on their faces. Children quickly pick up on tension and respond in kind.

Consider how you convey your expectations to your child and interact with her in general. Changing your style of communication might trigger cooperation and pleasant interactions rather than resistance and negative behavior from your child.

Providing Choices

Offering choices and providing children with more opportunities for control over tasks and situations can be an effective way of preventing problem behavior and encouraging positive behavior. There are a number of areas where parents might make decisions for children that they could be making for themselves. Providing more opportunities to make choices can build independence skills and foster good decision-making, as well as reduce problem behavior. Some examples of ways to provide choices to children are to allow them to decide:

- Which toys they want to play with

- Ways to organize their belongings

- The order of activities for the day

- Their own clothing (e.g., give choice of two outfits)

- Between meal or snack options

- The people with whom they interact

- To just say "no" once in a while

Parents might simply ask the child which item or activity she wants or create choice menus with written words or pictures for the child to pick from.

Prompting Good Behavior

Many children require help to know how to behave in particular circumstances. At first a child might need an explanation about what is expected in situations (e.g., "You must use your 'inside' voice when at the store"). Later on a child might still require prompts to remember to use this skill when actually in the situation. If a child does not require constant verbal prompts, written reminders or pictures can be useful. For example, pictures on storage boxes can show where toys should be placed. Establishing predictability, using schedules, and giving warnings can also be used to prompt good behavior.

To use these prevention strategies, parents must think, as well as act, proactively. This means anticipating difficult circumstances, considering all the options, and working out plans in advance. The preparations may not be just physical (i.e., what you do) but also mental (what you think).

Predictability

When a child faces a new situation, it helps to review expectations for behavior and explain what is going to happen next. Parents should clearly tell the child where they are going, who will be there, how long the child will stay, and exactly how they want the child to behave. It is important parents not assume that their children know how to do what they want them to do. Parents might have to be very clear with a child about the steps of sequences or skills required. The following social story is an example of how to clarify expectations for a child:

We are going to the park. When we get there, I need you to hold my hand while we are in the parking lot. You can climb on the jungle gym, swing, and run around the playground, but you must stay on the mulch. When it is time to leave the park, I want you to hold my hand again while we go to the car. Afterward, if you have followed these rules, we can stop for ice cream.

Scheduling

Written or visual schedules can help clarify upcoming events and activities. These can be useful if a child is younger, has difficulty with too much verbal information, or tends to get anxious (and display problem behavior) when routines change. These schedules might include pictures that illustrate the typical daily routines or drawings of special activities on a calendar. When routines have to change or the child is required to wait, these things may be indicated visually on the schedule (e.g., by moving the activity down the schedule).

Warnings

Some children have problems when an activity goes on too long or they have to wait. In this case, parents might warn them that the end is near (e.g., "We're almost done; I think you can stay in your seat and play with your toys for five more minutes"). Parents can also use timers or count downs (e.g., 3 minutes, 2 minutes, 1 minute) when nearing the end of an activity.

Case Example: Preventing Ben's Problem Behavior

Ben's parents used the following strategies to help prevent his problem behavior:

- *Set up a schedule with pictures of Ben's typical daily activities.*

- *Prior to transitions (starting about 15 minutes prior to leaving), remind him periodically of where he will be going by pointing to that picture on his schedule.*

- *Explain what he needs to do when transitioning (e.g., "When it is time to go, I will help you put away your toys, get your shoes on, and take your toy bag to the car). Remind him of fun things he can do or treats he will receive where he is going.*

- *Create a bag of special toys that Ben may take with him in the car when he goes somewhere, and place a few of his favorites in the glove compartment. Change out the toys periodically, and keep them only for transitions.*

- *Schedule several different play sessions during and after school, and include those sessions on Ben's schedule. Alternate playing with mom or teacher and playing independently (so that Ben can enjoy his time alone during play also). Make the sessions very short, with only small attempts to play with him (e.g., handing him a toy or simply playing with the toys next to him without asking anything of him). Tell him exactly what you want to do with him before play will be finished (e.g., "after we finish this puzzle together, I will let you play alone").*

- *Have Ben eat meals and snacks only at the table. Provide Ben with some of his favorite foods during breakfast and lunch (to encourage him to eat). Prior to starting to prepare a meal, get Ben involved in an activity he particularly likes to distract him from dinner preparation. Set the table ahead of time, and do whatever preparations can be done earlier in the day (when Ben is not hungry). When it's time to eat, bring him to the table explaining that he must sit to eat.*

Identifying Prevention Strategies

Recall the hypothesis or summary statement about your child that you developed in the last session. Record your ideas for avoiding or improving difficult situations, providing choices, and prompting good behavior on the Preventing

Problems Worksheet. You might want to refer back to your initial ideas for preventing problems in the left column of the Brainstorming Interventions form from Session 3. Consider how these strategies might be put in place.

Homework

✎ Continue to keep Self-Talk Journal.

✎ Practice using the disputation process to replace pessimistic beliefs.

✎ Complete the Weekly Progress Report.

✎ Complete the Preventing Problems Worksheet. Try some of these strategies, and observe the impact on your child's behavior (continue data collection using the methods selected in Sessions 1 and 2).

✎ Try to talk with family members and others to get their input on prevention strategies.

Preventing Problems Worksheet

Circumstances that set the stage for my child's behavior:

My strategies to prevent problems:
Avoid difficult situations:

Improve difficult situations:

Provide choices:

Prompt good behavior:

Of these strategies, what worked and what didn't?

Weekly Progress Report

Child: _____   Parent(s): _____

Our child's behaviors are now happening:

Behavior	Never	A few times	Almost every day	More than once per day	Many times per day	Almost every hour	Many times per hour

Other changes for our child and family: _____

_____

_____

Some new things we tried this week: _____

_____

_____

Session 5   *Managing Consequences*

Goals

- To use affirmations to replace pessimistic beliefs

- To understand how reactions may maintain your child's behavior

- To learn how to manage consequences

- To take precautions when using punishment

Using Affirmations

By now you should be able to identify inaccurate and unproductive thoughts. You have also learned how to stop these thoughts in process. At this point, it is beneficial to replace those beliefs with positive self-talk. This is called substitution or reattribution. In essence, you will want to replace your pessimistic ideas with affirmations. Examples of an affirmation include "This is a difficult situation, and I am handling it well" and "I am a committed, loving parent."

Affirmations should be:

- Stated in present tense (e.g., "I am a gentle, but firm, parent" vs. "I will be better next time")

- Focused on solutions, stating what can be done to resolve a situation (e.g., "I can explain calmly what I want him to do and guide him, if necessary")

- Both specific and comprehensive (i.e., clear and relate to various situations in which pessimistic beliefs are likely to arise)

- Honest and practical (i.e., not resulting in false impressions or unreasonable expectations)

Consider one or more of the entries in your Self-Talk Journal. What is something positive you could say to yourself in that situation? Record the affirmation

Self-Talk Journal – Session 5

Situation	Beliefs	Consequences	Disputation	Substitution	Comments
What happened (success or difficulty)?	What did you think or feel (self-talk)?	What happened as a result (actions)?	Was this a useful or accurate belief?	What is a more positive belief (affirmation)?	
When my son sat down for dinner, he started whining and crying. (difficulty)	I thought "I'm a bad mother, and I'm not able to control his behavior."	I gave him cookies so he would stop crying.	Is the belief true? Probably not. Are there other explanations? My son was hungry and tired. Is this belief helpful? No, it just makes me feel bad, and I give up trying.	I work hard at being a good mother and am able to get him to do some chores.	
			Is the belief true? Are there other explanations? Is this belief helpful?		
			Is the belief true? Are there other explanations? Is this belief helpful?		
			Is the belief true? Are there other explanations? Is this belief helpful?		

in column 5 of your Self-Talk Journal. You may photocopy this form as needed (see appendix for an additional copy).

Maintaining Problem Behavior

The consequences that result from behavior, including the way people react to the child, may maintain the problem behavior. In other words, if children get something they want or avoid something unpleasant, those results can increase the likelihood that the behavior will continue to occur. For example:

- Yelling or providing long explanations about why a behavior is a problem just after the incident can reinforce the behavior with attention (because any attention is better than none).

- Backing off from a demand because a child gets upset might cause the child to act up again to avoid or escape demands.

- Giving in to a request for a toy, food, or an activity because the child becomes increasingly demanding or disruptive will make that behavior worthwhile and more likely to occur in the future.

- Ignoring certain kinds of behavior to avoid giving attention can be counter-productive. If the behavior occurs because it feels, looks, or sounds good to the child (e.g., hand flapping), it might be more likely to continue if left alone.

Think about the results (including your own reactions) that your child's behavior produces and how those outcomes might be maintaining problem behavior. Ask yourself: How can I respond to my child's behavior so that he gets the results he desires more readily for good behavior than problem behavior?

Also consider what you may be saying to yourself at the moment the problem behavior is occurring. For example, you might think something like, "It doesn't matter what I do" or "Look how upset my child is; I should just give him what he wants." Explore how these kinds of thoughts might contribute to how you react.

Managing Consequences

Parents can change consequences to promote positive behavior and deter problem behavior. The ultimate goal when managing consequences is to make sure a child's goals are achieved through positive behavior rather than problem behavior.

Parents also must make sure their reactions are not actually feeding into the problem. Possible strategies include:

- If a child misbehaves for attention, ask other people to interact with the child only when he is behaving nicely. As soon as he begins to act out, they should stop looking at the child or commenting on his behavior.

- If a child acts up when he wants an activity, a toy, or other item, make sure those things are available for positive, but not problem, behavior. *Examples*: requiring the child to say or sign for something before receiving it; allowing treats only after finishing dinner.

- If a child seems to enjoy the behavior itself (i.e., it feels good), find other ways for the child to get that same kind of stimulation. *Examples*: dancing, manipulating toys instead of rocking and flapping hands.

- If a child behaves badly to escape something he doesn't like, give the child breaks or reduce demands when he is behaving appropriately. Otherwise, try not to allow the child to avoid those situations. *Examples*: allowing the child to leave a restaurant and go for a walk if he signals "out."

Obviously, you do not have control of every consequence of your child's behavior in every situation. For example, you cannot always stop the attention your child receives from other people for misbehavior. However, the things you can do will still produce positive change. For the most impact, strive to respond immediately when behaviors occur and to be as consistent as possible. For example, be sure to reward positive behavior immediately every time it happens.

Case Example: Responding to Ben's Behavior

Here are the strategies Ben's parents used to respond to his behavior. Note how they provide reinforcement when he engages in positive or replacement behavior and withhold reinforcement when he engages in problem behavior.

- *If Ben asks appropriately for a delay in a transition or a break from playing with someone (e.g., by putting his hand up, by pointing to a toy or puzzle piece, or by saying "go"), back off for one minute saying, "Okay, you need space; one more minute." (Allow some time in the schedule for these brief delays.)*

- *Praise Ben for transitioning and tolerating others participating in his play, and acknowledge it is hard for him. Praise every little action he does appropriately (e.g., standing, walking out the door, sitting in the car or with a person, taking a puzzle piece). Provide little rewards for going places and doing things without tantrums (e.g., a special activity at school, a treat on an errand, time to play by himself).*

■ *During a transition, if Ben refuses to leave or drops to the floor, guide him gently but firmly to leave. Do not allow his behavior to delay the transition. Ignore crying and screaming and do not comment on his behavior (e.g., "You're just being a baby" or "I'm sitting here whether you like it or not").*

■ *If he begins to cry or scream during play, encourage him to say "go" (e.g., "do you want me to go?") or put his hand up, helping him to do it if necessary, and then back away. After a brief period, re-enter his play, saying, "I just want to play for a bit" (e.g., just long enough to hand him a toy). If he handles play without crying and screaming for a short period (e.g., one minute), ask him if he would like to be alone, prompt him to say "go," and leave. Gradually extend the time he is expected to play before he can ask someone to go.*

Identifying Consequence Strategies

Using a hypothesis or summary statement you have developed for your child, identify the consequences that appear to be maintaining the problem behavior. Record your ideas for reinforcing positive behavior and avoiding rewarding problem behavior on the Managing Consequences Worksheet. You might want to refer back to your initial ideas for managing consequences in the center column of the Brainstorming Interventions form from Session 3. Consider how these strategies might be put in place.

Managing Consequences Worksheet

Consequences of My Child's Behavior
My child gets:

My child avoids:

Management Strategies
Reinforce positive behavior:

Avoid rewarding problem behavior:

Change my reactions to behavior:

Of these strategies, what worked and what didn't?

It is very common for parents to react negatively to behavior problems, especially when they are tired or frustrated. This may be an unplanned reaction – for example, yelling "stop that." Or it may be part of a punishment plan – for example, using long time-outs, spanking, or withholding favorite things. Either way, parents need to use caution. Keep the following points in mind.

- Although punishment might interrupt the behavior, and the child's initial response might be to stop being disruptive, usually the behavior problems return again in the same situation.

- Children often learn when they will be punished (for example, by Dad at home) and when they will not be punished (for example, at a relative's house); therefore, they misbehave more in some places.

- A child may comply or stop a behavior quickly (but temporarily) through punishment, reinforcing parents to use it again.

- When punishment becomes less effective, there is a tendency to use more severe forms (for example, yelling louder, spanking, or removing access to more and more favorite things). This escalation of punishment can be difficult to stop.

- Punishment focuses on what we want a child *not* to do, rather than what we want a child to do in these situations.

Homework

- ✎ Continue to keep Self-Talk Journal.

- ✎ Continue practicing distraction and/or disputation strategies.

- ✎ Develop and practice positive affirmations.

- ✎ Complete the Weekly Progress Report.

- ✎ Complete the Managing Consequences Worksheet. Try out these strategies, and observe the impact they have on the child's behavior (continue data collection using the methods selected in Sessions 1 and 2).

- ✎ Try to talk with family members and others to get their input on consequence strategies.

Weekly Progress Report

Child: _____   Parent(s): _____

Our child's behaviors are now happening:

Behavior	Never	A few times	Almost every day	More than once per day	Many times per day	Almost every hour	Many times per hour

Other changes for our child and family: _____

_____

_____

_____

Some new things we tried this week: _____

_____

_____

Session 6   *Replacing Behavior*

Goals

- To practice cognitive restructuring

- To select replacement behaviors for your child

- To teach your child skills

Cognitive Restructuring

You have now learned how to identify and replace negative thoughts. This entire process is called cognitive restructuring. Review your Self-Talk Journal for overall themes or patterns.

Consider the strategies you have been using—for example, distraction, disputation, and affirmations. Ask yourself:

- What is working well?

- What isn't working?

- How will I do things differently next time?

Record your impressions in the comments section of the Self-Talk Journal. You may photocopy this form as needed (see appendix for an additional copy).

Self-Talk Journal

Situation	Beliefs	Consequences	Disputation	Substitution	Comments
What happened (success or difficulty)?	What did you think or feel (self-talk)?	What happened as a result (actions)?	Was this a useful or accurate belief?	What is a more positive belief (affirmation)?	
			Is the belief true? Are there other explanations? Is this belief helpful?		
			Is the belief true? Are there other explanations? Is this belief helpful?		
			Is the belief true? Are there other explanations? Is this belief helpful?		

While a child's problem behavior is often frustrating and overwhelming, it is important for parents to recognize that the behavior is also purposeful. Children misbehave because, at the moment, they lack appropriate and effective skills to deal with unpleasant situations or to get what they want. Problem behavior is typically a child's way of telling other people that she needs something or wants something to stop.

This view of behavior is often difficult for parents to accept because they see their child's behavior as simply being a product of her disability. Or it can be hard for parents to understand or accept the purposes behavior is serving for their child. For example, a parent might be used to seeing a child's behavior as mean or defiant rather than as an effort to obtain attention or avoid difficult tasks. Parents of children with disabilities or behavioral challenges can also feel confused about their child's capability. They might set unrealistic expectations or underestimate their child's potential. If you find that you are experiencing some of these difficulties when identifying replacement behaviors, it is important to use your self-talk strategies to explore and address them. Realizing that problem behavior is a means to an end can help you find other more appropriate or desirable ways for your child to behave.

To help identify specific replacement behaviors, ask yourself: What else could my child do to get what she needs, to avoid or delay a difficult situation, or to deal with particular circumstances more appropriately and effectively?

Replacement behaviors could include requesting specific items, activities, or types of interactions; completing chores or other daily living tasks more independently; or simply learning to tolerate unpleasant circumstances for periods of time. For example:

- If a child misbehaves when uncomfortable or upset, teach the child how to address her own needs (e.g., breathe deeply when anxious, get a drink when thirsty).

- If a child has difficulty with certain activities, encourage her to ask for help, switch to another activity, or take periodic breaks.

- If a child acts out when wanting attention, teach her how to begin an interaction (e.g., by touching a person's hand or holding up a toy) or to get involved in another activity until a person becomes available.

- If a child usually responds to having to give up preferred items or toys with misbehavior (e.g., resisting putting away her favorite magazine), teach her how to appropriately ask for the things back, take turns sharing them with others, or put the items away herself.

In addition to trying some of these immediate ways of resolving problems and meeting needs, you might also want to teach your child other life skills such as:

- Social skills to use when interacting with other children (e.g., how to join play or take turns in a game)

- How to use toys or other items appropriately

- Self care such as grooming

- Leisure activities (e.g., hobbies) so the child can entertain herself for periods of time

Competing with Problem Behavior

Long-held habits can be difficult to change. Even as adults, our own patterns of behavior are hard to break. Likewise, a child who is used to being disruptive to communicate or to get her needs met might initially resist efforts to change her behavior and feel frustrated that behaviors that have worked previously are no longer working. For other, more appropriate, behavior to replace problem behaviors, the new behavior has to be easy for the child to use and produce the same or similar outcomes. That is, it has to compete effectively with the problem behavior. A child then learns that it may be easier to get what she wants by using the new behavior rather than the old inappropriate behavior. The "payoff" has to be as good or better for the new behavior to outweigh the benefits of using the problem behavior.

For example, a child's screaming when she doesn't get her way with her parents might be very effective because they "give in" immediately to stop the screaming. If the parents try to get the child to say in a full sentence "I want ____ please" and she has difficulty speaking, it will certainly be easier for her to scream. In this situation, it might be more appropriate to simplify the expectation and require the child only to point to the item. The parents could later expect her to say the word and then speak in a full sentence. This way the child can be immediately successful and will be more likely to communicate in an appropriate manner.

This concept of giving a child more appropriate ways to get her needs met might make a good deal of sense to parents, but it can also challenge their assumptions. For example, some parents believe children should behave nicely because it is the right thing to do, not because they get rewards for doing so. That belief system would make it difficult for them to encourage replacement skills and follow through with providing rewards. If you have assumptions that would interfere with using this approach, it is important to use the self-talk strategies to evaluate and replace them as needed.

Case Example: Replacing Ben's Problem Behavior

The following are ways Ben's parents taught him new behaviors to replace his problem behavior.

- *Encourage Ben to ask for a brief delay in transitions by putting his hand up or pointing to a puzzle piece (to indicate he wants to continue playing). To prompt him, say, "What do you want?" and physically guide him through the movement.*

- *Teach Ben to check his schedule prior to transitions. (The schedule will be posted near his play area where he has access to it at all times.) Have him put his puzzles or toys away prior to leaving.*

- *Have him practice waiting for food for brief periods of time and stopping activities to do something else (e.g., to wash his hands or wipe his mouth). Encourage Ben to ask to continue activities: say, "what do you want?" Help him point toward the activity and then say, "Oh, you want to play with the puzzle."*

- *Practice playing with Ben by initially sitting beside him, then touching his toys, then handing him toys he needs, and eventually taking turns with toys. Prompt him to say "go" or put his hand up when he needs a break, and move away.*

- *Have Ben practice eating at the table for short periods of time, providing praise and treats when he remains in his seat.*

Replacing My Child's Behavior

Using a hypothesis or summary statement you developed (see Session 3), think about both the function of the problem behavior and the circumstances precipitating it. Then identify skills that would replace the problem behavior. Remember that the replacement behaviors should achieve the same function as the problem

Replacing Behavior Worksheet

What is my child currently doing that is of concern?

What would I like my child to do instead ("replacement" behavior)?

behavior (and/or allow the child to cope better with the circumstances). The behaviors should be clearly defined and be efficient and effective. Record your ideas for new skills and behaviors on the Replacing Behavior Worksheet. You might want to refer back to your initial ideas for replacing behavior in the right column of the Brainstorming Interventions form from Session 3.

Teaching Skills

The most important long-term approach for addressing a child's behavior is to give her better ways to meet her needs and handle difficult situations. Positive behavior support is about teaching a child the skills she needs to be successful.

For many children, learning new behaviors takes more than simply showing them or describing what parents want them to do. Often times, new skills must be presented in a systematic way for them to be effectively learned. Parents can be effective teachers, following a sequence of strategies to build and reinforce these skills in their children. The following are the steps for teaching skills (see following case study for examples of each step):

Step 1. Identify what exactly you want to teach (i.e., what you want your child to say or do). Break it down into teachable units, and define the steps or components clearly. This is called a task analysis.

Step 2. Decide where, when, and with whom this skill is needed (e.g., when shopping in public, at meal times, or with grandparents).

Step 3. Arrange the environment to prompt the use of the skill and provide reminders, relying on natural cues whenever possible.

Step 4. Help your child to be successful in performing the skill by using effective prompting methods such as:

- Giving your child an example

- Showing your child how to do it

- Using gestures (e.g., pointing)

- Physically guiding your child through the behavior

Step 5. Praise and reward use of the skill or progress in the right direction. Correct errors, and withhold rewards following mistakes and resistance.

Step 6. Gradually reduce your assistance, your feedback, and the rewards you provide to lessen dependence. Use of the skill and the results it produces should become their own reward.

Case Study: Teaching Ben Skills

Ben's parents followed the six steps described in the previous section to teach Ben new skills and behaviors.

Step 1: Ben's parents identified that they wanted to teach Ben to transition from the house or classroom to the car by having Ben:

  1. *Put away toys and other materials*

  2. *Walk to his schedule and point to the picture indicating the next activity*

  3. *Put on his shoes (with assistance from his parent or teacher)*

  4. *Pick up his "car toys" bag and take it with him*

  5. *Walk calmly to the car and get in*

Step 2: Ben's parents decided this transitioning skill was needed any time Ben must leave one place to go to another (e.g., from home, school, or the store to the car).

Step 3: To provide cues for the skill, Ben's parents put a small bag of special car transition toys near the door but out of Ben's reach. They changed these toys periodically and whenever Ben seemed to lose interest in them. Prior to each transition, they would point to the bag and show Ben on his schedule where he would be going (e.g., "In a couple of minutes, we will be going to _____.") They also placed Ben's shoes near the play area with the Velcro undone. When it was time to leave, they would say, "Time for _____ (e.g., school, store)."

Step 4: Ben's parents showed Ben the behavior they wanted from him. Their plan was as follows:

  - *If Ben does not respond to "time for school" by putting away his toys, his parents model for him by putting one of his toys away for him and saying,"Your turn Ben; put away _____ (whatever toy he has)."*

  - *They wait for him to respond to the cue or prompt. If he still continues to play, they gesture and move the toy bin or container closer, saying "Put away _____ " (and pointing in the container).*

     ■   *If there is still no response, then they say, "I will help you Ben. This is hard. Put away _____," and guide Ben to drop the toy in the bin. If he does not drop it, they say "put away" and then pry the toy away and put it in the bin. "We can play later (after school)." Then they have Ben put on his shoes (or put them on for him) and get "car toys" bag.*

Step 5: *Ben's parents praised him frequently for putting his toys away (even if the toy had to be put in hand-over-hand), getting up and moving toward the door, picking up his toy bag, and leaving his shoes on (e.g., "Wow, you did it! You are walking with mommy"). If Ben made it to the car without a tantrum, they gave him an extra toy (kept in glove compartment). Once in the car, they said something every minute or two about sitting nicely in the car. When he arrived at his destination without a tantrum, they provided a special treat (e.g., fun activity at school, treat on the errand). They made a schedule to show him what he would get upon arrival to school. If Ben threw a tantrum, they continued the sequence described in Step 4 and made sure all toys got put away so there was complete closure to activities. They would say "one more puzzle piece or one more animal, then we go." They ignored screaming, crying, and dropping to the floor. They would say, "It is hard to stop playing. You can play later." They moved him through each step with as little delay as possible, reassuring him along the way.*

Step 6: *Ben's parents waited longer and longer (e.g., adding a few seconds each time) to praise or help Ben to put away his toys and get his shoes on. They praised him for spontaneously using his schedule. In the beginning, they limited transitions only to things Ben has to do (e.g., school) or really likes to do (e.g., swimming), then gradually added more activities.*

Teaching My Child Skills

Refer to the ideas you listed on the Replacing Behavior Worksheet. Consider which replacement behaviors require systematically teaching your child new skills. Starting with the skill you see as most important and urgently needed, work through the six steps, recording the information on the Teaching Plan form. A copy of the blank form can be found in an appendix at the back of the book. You may photocopy additional forms as needed.

Teaching Plan

Develop a plan for teaching a replacement skill to your child.

1. What exactly do you want your child to say or do (steps/components)?

2. Where, when, and with whom (under what circumstances) do you want your child to use this skill?

3. How will you arrange the environment or provide reminders to prompt your child to use this skill?

4. What prompting methods (e.g., describing, showing, gestures, physical guidance) will you use to help your child use the skill?

5. How will you reward your child for using the skill (or making progress in the right direction) and respond to errors when they occur?

6. How will you gradually reduce your assistance and reinforcement over time (to transfer control to your child)?

Homework

✎ Continue to keep Self-Talk Journal.

✎ Continue practicing distraction, disputation, and positive affirmations.

✎ Complete the Weekly Progress Report.

✎ Complete the Replacing Behavior Worksheet.

✎ Complete Teaching Plan form(s).

✎ Try out the strategies for replacing behavior and teaching skills, and observe the impact they have on the child's behavior (continue data collection using the methods selected in Sessions 1 and 2).

✎ Try to talk with family members and others to get their input on replacing behavior and teaching skills.

Weekly Progress Report

Child: _____   Parent(s): _____

Our child's behaviors are now happening:

Behavior	Never	A few times	Almost every day	More than once per day	Many times per day	Almost every hour	Many times per hour

Other changes for our child and family: _____

_____

_____

Some new things we tried this week: _____

_____

_____

Session 7

Putting the Behavior Support Plan in Place

Goals

- To review self-talk and apply cognitive strategies

- To design a behavior support plan

- To make sure the behavior support plan fits

- To improve your child's and family's lives

- To create an action plan

Self-Talk Review and Application

Now that you have learned the process of cognitive restructuring, it is important to continue to review your self-talk and evaluate your use of strategies. Review your Self-Talk Journal, and look for themes or patterns. Evaluate how you are doing with your self-talk. What is working well? What isn't working? How will you do things differently next time? Record your impressions in the comments section of your Self-Talk Journal. You may photocopy this form as needed (see appendix for an additional copy).

Keep practicing identifying any negative thoughts or feelings, circumstances that precipitate them, and consequences of those beliefs. Continue to use disputation and/or distraction, and substitute pessimistic thoughts with positive affirmations.

Self-Talk Journal

Situation What happened (success or difficulty)?	Beliefs What did you think or feel (self-talk)?	Consequences What happened as a result (actions)?	Disputation Was this a useful or accurate belief?	Substitution What is a more positive belief (affirmation)?	Comments
			Is the belief true? Are there other explanations? Is this belief helpful?		
			Is the belief true? Are there other explanations? Is this belief helpful?		
			Is the belief true? Are there other explanations? Is this belief helpful?		

It is important to develop a comprehensive written behavior support plan. Having this in hand will help put the plan in place and ensure that it will be used consistently. Though it might seem that the plan should fall naturally into place at this point, there are issues that will influence how well it is carried out and how effective it will be. These issues include:

- The clarity of the plan

- The degree to which the strategies fit your child and family

- The degree to which the plan produces positive lifestyle changes

- The specific steps taken to put the plan into action

Integrating Components

Written behavior support plans are important because they help everyone involved communicate. They can be reviewed frequently to keep interventions on course and revised as changes become necessary. Behavior support plans should be based on the summary statements generated during information gathering and pattern analysis. A good behavior support plan includes the following components:

1. Strategies to prevent behavior problems (e.g., avoiding difficult circumstances, making situations better, adding prompts for good behavior)

2. Strategies for managing consequences (i.e., making sure that rewards are provided for positive behavior and not problem behavior)

3. Strategies for systematically teaching replacement skills so that the child's needs can be met through more appropriate means where and when they are needed

Case Example: Behavior Support Plan for Ben

See the example of a behavior support plan for the case study in Figure 7.1. Note that the plan includes goals, target behaviors, summary statements, strategies for preventing problems, strategies for managing consequences, skills for teaching replacement behavior, and a monitoring plan.

Behavior Support Plan: Part 1

Child's Name: Ben	Date: 10/1/07

Team Members: Who is involved in the process?

Ben's parents, his grandmother, and his preschool teacher (also include friends at school and in neighborhood and babysitter)

Intervention Settings: Where will the plan be used?

Home, school, community outings

Description of Problem Behavior: What does the child say or do?	**Baseline Estimate:** How often? How long?
Tantrums: screaming, crying, dropping to the floor	5 times per day

Broad Goals: How would you like life to improve for your child and family?

Ben will play with other children and adults, handle transitions and change better, and ride in the car and eat with the family without problem behavior.

Ben will develop more interests (beyond animals and puzzles) and participate in typical childhood experiences, including spending time with friends.

Ben will become more independent with his self-care, sleep alone, and develop the skills he needs to keep himself safe (e.g., looking out for traffic).

Ben's parents will be able to enjoy life as a family without the constant stress presented by his problem behavior. They hope to be able to go places and do more things as a family and to reduce the conflict in their lives.

Summary Statements: Describe circumstances, behavior, and consequences (get/avoid).

When Ben's parents try to put his shoes on to leave the house, Ben screams, cries, and drops to the floor. This delays the transition, forces his mother to take him out without shoes, or results in her canceling the errand or getting someone else to do it.

When his parents or peers try to play with Ben, he screams and cries; if they don't back off, he turns his back on them or pushes them away. Eventually, the children or family members back off, and Ben is able to continue playing contentedly by himself.

When Ben doesn't eat well at breakfast and lunch, he screams and cries as dinnertime approaches. If Ben's mother doesn't feed him right away, he might bang his head. As a result, she quickly prepares him something he likes to eat. She often allows Ben to carry his food around (rather than requiring him to sit with the family during meals).

Figure 7.1

Example of Completed Behavior Support Plan

Behavior Support Plan: Part 2

Intervention Components: What strategies will be used (based on the summary statements)?

Prevention: What changes will be made to avoid problems, make difficult situations better, or prompt good behavior?	**Management:** How will you respond to reward positive behavior and not problem behavior?	**Replacement:** What skills will be taught to replace the problem behavior?
Set up a schedule with pictures of Ben's typical daily activities. Prior to transitions, remind him of where he will be going by pointing to that picture on his schedule.	If Ben asks for a delay in a transition or a break from play appropriately, back of for one minute, saying, "okay, you need space/one minute."	Encourage Ben to ask for a brief delay in transitions by putting his hand up or pointing to a toy (to indicate he wants to continue play). To prompt him, say, "What do you want?" and guide him through the movement.
Explain what he needs to do during the transition, using consistent words. Remind him of fun things he can do or treats he will receive where he is going.	Praise Ben for transitioning and tolerating others playing with him. Praise every action he does well. Provide small rewards for going places and doing things without tantrums.	Teach Ben to check his schedule prior to transitions. Have him put his toys away prior to leaving.
Create a bag of special toys that Ben may take with him on outings, and place a few of his favorites in the glove compartment. Change out the toys periodically, and keep them only for transitions.	During a transition, if Ben refuses to leave or drops to the floor, guide him gently but firmly to leave. Do not delay the transition. Ignore crying and screaming.	Have Ben practice waiting for food for brief periods of time and stopping activities to do something else. Encourage Ben to ask to continue by saying to him, "what do you want?" Help him point toward the activity and then say, "Oh, you want to play with puzzle/animals."
Schedule play sessions during and after school. Alternate playing with others and playing independently. Make the sessions very short, with only small attempts to play with him or simply playing with the toys next to him without demands. Tell him exactly what you want to do with him before ending playtime.	If he plays without crying and screaming for a short period, ask him if he would like to be alone, prompt him to say "go," and leave. Gradually extend the time he is expected to play before asking someone to go. If he begins to cry or scream during play, remain in the area until he asks "go."	Teach Ben to tolerate play with other people by sitting beside him, touching his toys, handing him toys, and eventually taking turns with the toys. Prompt him to say "go" or put his hand up when he needs a break.
Have Ben eat meals and snacks only at the table.	Allow Ben to leave the table during meals, but ask him to put his food down before he goes. If he	Have Ben practice eating at the table for short periods of time.

Figure 7.1 *continued*

Behavior Support Plan: Part 2

Intervention Components: *continued*		
Provide Ben with some of his favorite foods during breakfast and lunch. Before meal preparation, get Ben involved in an activity. (Set the table ahead of time, and do whatever preparations can be done earlier in the day). When it's time to eat, bring him to the table explaining that he must sit to eat.	refuses, remove the food. When he is seated, return the food. Reward Ben for eating at the table with his favorite foods.	Teach Ben daily living skills, such as tooth brushing and potty training.

Crisis Management:

Is a plan needed to ensure the safety of your child, other people, and the surroundings?
__X__ yes____ no

If so, describe strategies:

If necessary, physically guide or carry Ben out of public places or unsafe situations—being careful to be gentle but firm.

Other Support: What else can improve life for your child and your family?

Take Ben out to new places (e.g., a water park, playground, convenience store) periodically.

Find peers in the neighborhood and at school to play with Ben weekly; teach the children how to enter his play without upsetting him.

Develop a plan for teaching Ben to use the potty (e.g., creating a schedule, using rewards) and self-care skills (e.g., washing hands). Institute a regular bedtime routine.

Locate a babysitter for weekend dates. Become involved in a support group in the community.

Figure 7.1 *continued*

Behavior Support Plan: Part 3

Action Plan Steps		
Steps to be taken:	Person responsible:	Time to be completed by:
Review the plan and get a commitment from other people who care for Ben (e.g., family members, teachers) to carry out the plan.	Mom	10/7
Create a picture schedule for home and school (take pictures, purchase supplies, and laminate).	Mom and Teacher	10/14
Get oversized bag and new toys for outings.	Dad and Grandma	10/14

Monitoring:

How often will the plan be monitored? _X_ daily _X_ weekly ____monthly ____ other

How will implementation and outcomes be evaluated?

Continue using scatterplot and ABC recording forms to evaluate changes in behavior. Keep a daily journal that includes particularly successful and unsuccessful transitions, results of attempts to play with Ben, and estimated times Ben remains at the dinner table. Meet briefly with Ben's teacher at the end of the school day on Fridays to discuss progress and decide on changes to be made.

Monitoring methods (e.g., forms): Scatterplot, Behavior Log

Figure 7.1 *continued*

As you develop the behavior support plan, there may be a variety of possible strategies to choose from. For example, there may be numerous ways to prevent problems from occurring or several specific behaviors that may be identified as replacement skills. Select those strategies that best fit your child's and family's needs, skills, strengths, challenges, and goals. Discuss your concerns and ideas with your child and other family members to get their input whenever possible.

Once you have designed the plan, you will need to determine whether it is really "doable," acceptable to everyone involved, and fits with your family. Consider the following questions:

1. Does my team have enough time to put this in place?

2. Does my team have the energy to use it consistently?

3. Does my team have the resources we need to make it work?

4. Does the plan fit given my family's values and needs?

5. Does the plan work within typical family routines?

6. Does everyone believe in the plan and agree to use it?

At this point, it is also important to revisit your self-talk associated with implementing the plan. When you think about using the strategies, are you fully committed or do you still have reservations? If you have reservations, what exactly are they? If they are practical concerns, the plan should be altered. If they are not productive beliefs, you should use distraction, disputation, and/or substitution to address them.

Case Example: Making Ben's Plan Fit

See the following case example, and refer to the corresponding Behavior Support Plan in Figure 7.1. Note any factors that would affect the design or implementation of the plan.

The primary challenges for Ben's family were getting everyone on the same page (including Grandma) and managing all the individual tasks associated with his plan. It was important to make sure that everyone had the same goals and expectations and was adequately supported. Ben's team (parents, grandma, and teacher) agreed to meet and go over the plan together, discussing any concerns, making sure everyone understood what he or she was doing and why, and making adjustments to the plan as needed to ensure buy-in. Then they all promised to follow through and communicate openly about their concerns as time went by. They also discussed the fact that it might take time for the plan to work and that they all needed to be patient. Ben's mom talked to his teacher about how overwhelmed she was with trying to create his schedule. His teacher agreed to help Mom put it together after school while Dad watched Ben. Ben's mom found that trying to carry all of the different items to the car was difficult, so she bought an oversized bag to use during transitions.

Promoting Lifestyle Change

The primarily goal of positive behavior support is not just to diminish problems but also to promote positive lifestyle change. If broader "life issues" are affecting your child's behavior, these will need to be addressed to produce positive changes. For example, if a child is generally dissatisfied with the types of activities or circle of friends with whom he interacts, those circumstances will produce worse overall behavior. Some questions you might want to think about are:

1. Are there physical or medical conditions that need to be addressed?

2. Is my child allowed to make choices and exert control over important aspects of his life?

3. Do my child's current schedule and daily routines match his preferred style?

4. Are there aspects of my child's surroundings that need to be changed?

5. Does my child have positive, non-instructional interactions (i.e., simply playing without placing demands on the child) with other people?

Considering these questions, you might be able to make some broad adjustments to your child's life that will improve his overall behavior—and even make using the other strategies less necessary. Also consider how you can improve family life for everyone—yourself included.

Making life changes can be particularly hard when parents have preconceived expectations about their child, life, and future. For example, it might be necessary to allow a child more freedom and independence (e.g., to visit a neighbor, try to ride a bicycle). These types of changes can be frightening for parents if there are risks involved. It may require parents to lean on other people more so they can better meet their own needs. Parents may also need to change their overall vision regarding how life should be or what the future holds. If preconceptions emerge when your family is considering life changes, these beliefs should be explored and addressed.

Case Example: Improving Ben's Life

The following describes strategies for the case study directed at improving the broader quality of life for Ben and his family. Note how the plan relates to independence, community participation, and relationships. Refer to the corresponding example of a Behavior Support Plan for Ben in Figure 7.1.

- *Ben's parents decided to start trying to take Ben out to new places (e.g., a water park, playground, convenience store) once in a while to expose him to new things. They also found a child from the neighborhood who was willing to come over once a week to play with or around Ben; Ben's mom taught the child how to enter his play without upsetting him. The same was done at school by his teacher with a child from another class.*

- *Ben's parents and teacher worked together to develop a plan for teaching him to use the potty (e.g., creating a schedule, using rewards), and they identified self-care skills (e.g., washing hands) they could teach together using the steps for teaching skills described in Session 4. His parents also instituted a regular bedtime routine to create a more consistent, positive transition to bed at night.*

- *Ben's parents were able to find an assistant at Ben's preschool who was willing to babysit periodically so that they could go out on dates together. They also became involved in a support group in the community so that they could foster relationships with other families and get support when they needed it.*

Behavior Support Plan for My Child

Over the last six sessions, you have established your child's team, identified goals and target behaviors, developed hypotheses, and brainstormed interventions. Look over material from the previous sessions to complete the Behavior Support Plan for your child. As you complete the form, make sure the plan fits with your family and includes strategies for lifestyle change. Remember the goal is to have a plan that works well for everyone involved and improves the lives of your child and family. An additional blank Behavior Support Plan can be found in an appendix at the back of the book. You may photocopy the form as needed.

Behavior Support Plan: Part 1

Child's Name:	Date:

Team Members: Who is involved in the process?

Intervention Settings: Where will the plan be used?

Description of Problem Behavior: What does the child say or do?	**Baseline Estimate:** How often? How long?

Broad Goals: How would you like life to improve for your child and family?

Summary Statements: Describe circumstances, behavior, and consequences (get/avoid).

Behavior Support Plan: Part 2

Intervention Components: What strategies will be used (based on the summary statements)?		
Prevention: What changes will be made to avoid problems, make difficult situations better, or prompt good behavior?	**Management:** How will you respond to reward positive behavior and not problem behavior?	**Replacement:** What skills will be taught to replace the problem behavior?

Crisis Management:

Is a plan needed to ensure the safety of your child, other people, and the surroundings? __yes__no
If so, describe strategies:

Other Support: What else can improve life for your child and your family?

Behavior Support Plan: Part 3

Action Plan Steps		
Steps to be taken:	Person responsible:	Time to be completed by:

Monitoring:

How often will the plan be monitored?   __ daily   __ weekly   __ monthly   __ other:

How will implementation and outcomes be evaluated?

Monitoring methods (e.g., forms):

Once a behavior support plan has been developed, certain steps need to be taken to implement the plan with some degree of consistency. Consistency is important because "hit and miss" use of behavioral strategies could sometimes end up reinforcing problem behaviors and actually making them worse. To get the plan in place, it might be necessary to line up support from extended family, friends, babysitters, or teachers. Parents may need to consider how to draw in extra assistance for times that are too difficult to handle alone. Preparations might also include changing schedules, setting up methods to record changes in behavior over time, rearranging things at home, or making other modifications that can reduce some of the stress associated with implementing the plan. Setting the plan into motion can feel overwhelming; however, careful planning and assignment of responsibility can make follow-through easier.

Case Example: Action Plan Steps for Ben

Refer to the Action Plan for Ben included in the sample Behavior Support Plan in Figure 7.1. Note that the action plan includes what will be done, by whom, when, and/or how. Ben's parents identified the following action steps:

1. *Review the plan and get a commitment from other people who care for Ben (e.g., family members, teachers) to carry out the plan.*

2. *Work with Ben's teacher to create a schedule for home and school that includes transitions and play times. Decide beforehand who will get what materials (e.g., Ben's mother will get poster board, pictures of settings or things that can represent activities for home, toys for the bag, and some other reward to leave with the teacher; teacher will take photographs of activities at school, get pictures of possible rewards, and laminate the schedule for home and school).*

3. *Continue using the data collection procedures (scatterplot and ABC recording) to monitor and evaluate how the plan is working.*

4. *Meet briefly at the end of the school day on Fridays to discuss progress and decide on changes to be made.*

My Action Plan

Identify the action steps that need to be implemented, and record them under "Action Plan Steps" on Part 3 of the Behavior Support Plan form.

Homework

✎ Continue to keep Self-Talk Journal.

✎ Continue practicing distraction, disputation, and positive affirmations.

✎ Complete the Weekly Progress Report.

✎ Complete the Behavior Support Plan, including developing action plan steps for implementing the behavior support plan.

✎ Try to talk with family members and others to get their input on behavior support plan and action plan steps.

Weekly Progress Report

Child: _____   Parent(s): _____

Our child's behaviors are now happening:

Behavior	Never	A few times	Almost every day	More than once per day	Many times per day	Almost every hour	Many times per hour

Other changes for our child and family: _____

_____

_____

Some new things we tried this week: _____

_____

_____

Session 8 *Monitoring Results and Wrap-up*

Goals

- ▨ To review self-talk and continue to apply cognitive strategies

- ▨ To make a monitoring plan

- ▨ To learn how to make adjustments over time

- ▨ To complete the training and continue on your own

Self-Talk Review and Application

Review all your Self-Talk Journal sheets from the past seven weeks and look for general themes and patterns. Evaluate how you are doing with your self-talk strategies. What is working well? What isn't working? How will you do things differently next time? Record your impressions in the comments section of the Self-Talk Journal.

As this is the last session, it is important to identify strategies to maintain positive changes in self-talk. After the training has ended, you will continue evaluating and addressing your self-talk on your own. Be sure to keep using the following skills:

- ▨ Identifying situations, beliefs, and consequences

- ▨ Using distraction and/or disputation to challenge beliefs

- ▨ Substituting pessimistic self-talk with positive affirmations

A copy of the Self-Talk Journal is provided in an appendix. You may photocopy additional forms as needed.

Self-Talk Journal

Situation What happened (success or difficulty)?	Beliefs What did you think or feel (self-talk)?	Consequences What happened as a result (actions)?	Disputation Was this a useful or accurate belief?	Substitution What is a more positive belief (affirmation)?	Comments
			Is the belief true? Are there other explanations? Is this belief helpful?		
			Is the belief true? Are there other explanations? Is this belief helpful?		
			Is the belief true? Are there other explanations? Is this belief helpful?		

It is important to monitor the results of behavior support plans to make sure the strategies are working. Evaluating progress objectively often requires continuing to collect data. Sometimes changes in behavior can be subtle or take some time to occur. Also perceptions about how a plan is working might not necessarily match reality. It can be very helpful to review the progress across several weeks or even months and note changes that might not be obvious on a day-to-day basis. A system for recording and reviewing results can provide families with the positive feedback necessary to continue with the plan.

Remember, the goals of PBS include not only reductions in problem behaviors but also broader outcomes related to your child's and family's quality of life. Here are some questions to ask when monitoring results:

- Are my child's problem behaviors decreasing in frequency or intensity?

- Is my child using replacement behaviors appropriately and more than before?

- Is my family achieving the lifestyle-change goals established in these sessions?

- Is the behavior support plan still effective and reasonable for my child and family?

The specific methods used to monitor these results can be quite simple or more complex, as described in Session 1. For example, you might use simple frequency counts to evaluate changes in behaviors of concern, or you may use ratings or estimates of how well or often replacement skills are used (e.g., 4 out of 5). For behaviors that occur less often (e.g., once or twice a day), you can just take note of when they occur. However, if problems occur more frequently or they seem to be very complicated, it may be beneficial to create a more involved recording system. Consider having everyone involved in using the plan meet periodically. You can then look at the goals and target behaviors together to evaluate broader outcomes.

Your team will need to decide how often to review the plan and outcomes. Generally, this should be based on how often problems occurred before the plan was implemented. For example, if a child was hitting others on a daily basis, parents would want to review the data more often than for a child who had weekly tantrums.

It is very easy for parents to convince themselves that a plan is working or not working based on how they are thinking or feeling instead of judging the plan on the objective evidence. When parents feel discouraged, they might see the plan and themselves as less effective. To avoid this pattern, evaluate your self-talk, get input from other people, and rely on your monitoring system to evaluate outcomes.

Case Example: Monitoring the Behavior Support Plan for Ben

The following is how Ben's parents monitored their plan to evaluate its effectiveness over time. Note that it includes specific monitoring strategies and a schedule.

Ben's parents kept:

- *A daily journal including when, where, and with whom Ben made transitions and his accompanying problem behaviors*

- *A brief log of their attempts to play with Ben (i.e., what they were able to do with him)*

- *An estimate of how long he remained seated with the family for dinner each night*

Monitoring the Behavior Support Plan for My Child

Review the data you have collected to this point (see completed recording forms and Weekly Progress Reports). Using the Monitoring Plan Worksheet, develop a plan for monitoring how the behavior support plan is used and its outcomes. Also consider when and how you will communicate with your family and others involved in your child's care to assess progress.

After completing the Monitoring Plan Worksheet, you might want to use the Monitoring Form included at the end of this chapter to track the results of the behavior support plan. An additional blank form can be found in an appendix at the back of the book. You may photocopy the form as needed.

Monitoring Plan

What will I do to monitor the results of my child's plan?

How will I communicate with my family and others about our progress?

How often will we review how we are doing and make adjustments as needed?

Positive behavior support is an ongoing, problem-solving approach. It is not a quick fix parents do once and forget about. To be successful, plans must be used consistently over time and modified as needs arise. While initially it is important to be patient and not change the behavior support plan too quickly, if significant improvements have failed to occur after several weeks, the plan should be revisited. Even the best plans occasionally need to be modified.

All those using the plan should be continually asking themselves what is working and what is not and adjusting the plan as needed. As a child continues to develop, her needs and the situations affecting her behavior will change. Families might also go through transitions or life experiences that throw a wrench into the works. Changes in routines, circumstances, or life in general can prompt changes in a child's behavior.

It is important for parents to take note of such changes and the impact they have on a child's behavior, and be prepared to deal with them. Better yet, parents can try to anticipate and prepare for changes, avoiding unnecessary problems when possible. For example, a parent might take her child to visit a new classroom and identify a peer buddy to assist her or provide the teacher with a copy of the behavior support plan in advance. You can use the framework of PBS and its tools over and over, repeating the process whenever it's needed. In this way, you can effectively support your child as she encounters new situations and phases of her life.

Case Example: Outcomes of Ben's Plan

In the following case example, note the types of changes that occurred over time.

■ *Within three weeks of putting the plan in place, Ben's screaming and crying during most transitions decreased just to whining and occurred only about three times per week (and no longer than 30 seconds each time). When Ben started speech therapy, however, transitions again became a problem. When Ben knew he was headed to speech therapy at either home or school, his tantrums escalated in severity and were much longer. His parents, teachers, and therapists met to discuss this concern. They reviewed the circumstances surrounding his behavior and possible consequences. They determined that speech was particularly difficult for Ben and decided to make some changes to reduce the demands. The strategies included starting thera-py sessions with activities they knew to be easier for Ben, giving Ben periodic breaks, and adding special rewards when he transitioned and participated well. These strategies were quite successful.*

During play times, his mother and teacher were now able to sit with him while he was playing and pick up and hand him toys. He usually allowed them to remain with him for about two to three minutes before saying "go." He still wandered around the dinner table, but he began putting his food down before leaving with-out reminders. His parents were hopeful that he would start sitting with the family before long. Ben even looked at his schedule and put his toys away spontaneously. He seemed to enjoy the predictability of knowing where he was going and what would happen when he got there. Because of these improvements, his parents felt confident beginning to expose Ben to new people and places and tackling new skills such as sleeping alone and potty training. ▩

Making Adjustment to the Plan for My Child

Consider new behaviors of concern or upcoming events, changes, or transitions that might influence your child's behavior and/or the appropriateness of the cur-rent plan. Think about how the PBS process could be used to address those issues.

Also, identify one or more ways you can continually assess the plan, resolve prob-lems, and make adjustments as needed. Record this information on the Monitoring Plan Worksheet.

Conclusion

Congratulations on completing the program! Over the course of this training you have learned how:

▩ Self-talk affects the way a person feels and acts.

▩ Replacing pessimistic beliefs with positive affirmations allows parents to fol-low through with interventions and cope more effectively with challenges.

▩ PBS is collaborative—all those involved in a child's life should work together.

- PBS begins with an understanding of the circumstances that affect the child's behavior and the purposes the behavior serves for the child.

- Sometimes problem behavior can be prevented by

  - Anticipating difficult situations.

  - Avoiding or changing aspects of those situations.

  - Prompting the child to behave more appropriately.

- Parents can manage their reactions so that they provide their children with rewards for positive, and not problem, behavior.

- The most important element of a behavior support plan is to replace problem behavior by teaching a child appropriate skills to meet her needs.

- Behavior support plans should be clear, reasonable, and focused on important goals.

- To be effective, behavior support plans must be used consistently by all those involved.

- Behavior support plans must be monitored objectively on an ongoing basis to determine their effectiveness and recognize when adjustments are necessary.

You have probably already seen improvements in your child's behavior and life as a result of your participation in this program. It is important that you keep learning about how to best support your child. Continue monitoring your child's behavior, using PBS strategies, and evaluating your self-talk. Refer to the appendix at the back of this workbook for additional resources.

Monitoring Form

Our child's behaviors are now happening:

	Never	A few times	Almost every day	More than once per day	Many times per day	Almost every hour	Many times per hour
Problem Behavior							
New Skills							

What other positive or negative changes have occurred for our child and family (e.g., can we go more places or do more things)? _____

_____

_____

_____

_____

_____

Are the strategies included in our behavior plan being used consistently?   Yes   No

Are the strategies included in our behavior plan effective for our child?   Yes   No

Are the strategies included in our behavior plan right for our family?   Yes   No

If the answer is no to any of the previous questions, what kinds of changes do we need to make for the behavior plan to be more effective? _____

_____

_____

_____

_____

_____

PBS Resources for Parents

Books

Carr, E. G., Levin, L., McConnachie, G., Carlson, J. I., Kemp, D. C., & Smith, C. E. (1994). *Communication-based intervention for problem behavior: A user's guide for producing positive change.* Baltimore, MD: Paul H. Brookes Publishing.

Durand, V. M. (1998). *Sleep better! A guide to improving sleep for children with special needs.* Baltimore, MD: Paul H. Brookes Publishing.

Hieneman, M., Childs, K. E., & Sergay, J. (2006). *Parenting with positive behavior support: A practical guide to resolving your child's difficult behavior.* Baltimore, MD: Paul H. Brookes Publishing.

Koegel, L. K., Koegel, R. L., & Dunlap, G. (1996). *Positive behavior support: Including people with difficult behavior in the community.* Baltimore, MD: Paul H. Brookes Publishing.

Lucyshyn, J. M., Dunlap, G., & Albin, R. W. (2002). *Families and positive behavior support: Addressing problem behavior in family contexts.* Baltimore, MD: Paul H. Brookes Publishing.

O'Neill, R. E., Horner, R. H., Albin, R. W., Sprague, J. R., Storey, K., & Newton, J. S. (1997). *Functional assessment and program development for problem behavior: A practical handbook.* Pacific Grove, CA: Brooks/Cole.

Scotti, J. R., & Meyer, L. H. (1999). *Behavioral intervention: Principles, models, and practices.* Baltimore, MD: Paul H. Brookes Publishing.

Web Sites

Association for Positive Behavior Support (www.apbs.org)

Beach Center on Disability/PBS Program (www.beachcenter.org/pbs/default.aspx)

Center for Evidence-Based Practice: Young Children with Challenging Behavior (www.challengingbehavior.org)

Center on the Social and Emotional Foundations for Early Learning (www.vanderbilt.edu/csefel)

OSEP Center on Positive Behavioral Interventions and Supports (www.pbis.org)

Kansas Institute for Positive Behavior Support (www.kipbs.org)
Florida's Positive Behavior Support Project (http://flpbs.fmhi.usf.edu)
Colorado Positive Behavior Support Initiative (www.cde.state.co.us/pbs)
Positive Behavior Support—Nevada (www.pbsnv.org)

Additional Blank Forms

Self-Talk Journal

Situation	Beliefs	Consequences	Disputation	Substitution	Comments
What happened (success or difficulty)?	What did you think or feel (self-talk)?	What happened as a result (actions)?	Was this a useful or accurate belief?	What is a more positive belief (affirmation)?	
			Is the belief true? Are there other explanations? Is this belief helpful?		
			Is the belief true? Are there other explanations? Is this belief helpful?		
			Is the belief true? Are there other explanations? Is this belief helpful?		

Self-Talk Journal

Situation What happened (success or difficulty)?	Beliefs What did you think or feel (self-talk)?	Consequences What happened as a result (actions)?	Disputation Was this a useful or accurate belief?	Substitution What is a more positive belief (affirmation)?	Comments
			Is the belief true? Are there other explanations? Is this belief helpful?		
			Is the belief true? Are there other explanations? Is this belief helpful?		
			Is the belief true? Are there other explanations? Is this belief helpful?		

Counting Behaviors

Child: _____   Behavior: _____

Date	Start Time	Stop Time	Tallies	Total

Counting Behaviors

Child: _____   Behavior: _____

Date	Start Time	Stop Time	Tallies	Total

Timing Behaviors

Child: _____   Behavior: _____

Date	Time Behavior Started	Time Behavior Stopped	Total Time

Timing Behaviors

Child: _____   Behavior: _____

Date	Time Behavior Started	Time Behavior Stopped	Total Time

Rating Behaviors

Child: _____   Behavior: _____

Rating: 3 = severe   2 = moderate   1 = mild   0 = did not occur

Date	Time/Activity	Behavior Rating	Comments
		3 2 1 0	
		3 2 1 0	
		3 2 1 0	
		3 2 1 0	
		3 2 1 0	
		3 2 1 0	
		3 2 1 0	
		3 2 1 0	
		3 2 1 0	
		3 2 1 0	
		3 2 1 0	
		3 2 1 0	
		3 2 1 0	

Rating Behaviors

Child: _____   Behavior: _____

Rating: 3 = severe   2 = moderate   1 = mild   0 = did not occur

Date	Time/Activity	Behavior Rating				Comments
		3	2	1	0	
		3	2	1	0	
		3	2	1	0	
		3	2	1	0	
		3	2	1	0	
		3	2	1	0	
		3	2	1	0	
		3	2	1	0	
		3	2	1	0	
		3	2	1	0	
		3	2	1	0	
		3	2	1	0	
		3	2	1	0	

Frequency Graph

Child: _____   Behavior: _____

Each day, circle the number of times the behavior occurred. Draw a line from one circled number to the next to create a graph.

10	10	10	10	10	10	10	10	10	10	10	10	10	10
9	9	9	9	9	9	9	9	9	9	9	9	9	9
8	8	8	8	8	8	8	8	8	8	8	8	8	8
7	7	7	7	7	7	7	7	7	7	7	7	7	7
6	6	6	6	6	6	6	6	6	6	6	6	6	6
5	5	5	5	5	5	5	5	5	5	5	5	5	5
4	4	4	4	4	4	4	4	4	4	4	4	4	4
3	3	3	3	3	3	3	3	3	3	3	3	3	3
2	2	2	2	2	2	2	2	2	2	2	2	2	2
1	1	1	1	1	1	1	1	1	1	1	1	1	1
0	0	0	0	0	0	0	0	0	0	0	0	0	0

Frequency Graph

Child: _____   Behavior: _____

Each day, circle the number of times the behavior occurred. Draw a line from one circled number to the next to create a graph.

	10	10	10	10	10	10	10	10	10	10	10	10	10
	9	9	9	9	9	9	9	9	9	9	9	9	9
	8	8	8	8	8	8	8	8	8	8	8	8	8
	7	7	7	7	7	7	7	7	7	7	7	7	7
	6	6	6	6	6	6	6	6	6	6	6	6	6
	5	5	5	5	5	5	5	5	5	5	5	5	5
	4	4	4	4	4	4	4	4	4	4	4	4	4
	3	3	3	3	3	3	3	3	3	3	3	3	3
	2	2	2	2	2	2	2	2	2	2	2	2	2
	1	1	1	1	1	1	1	1	1	1	1	1	1
	0	0	0	0	0	0	0	0	0	0	0	0	0

Interview Form

Use the following questions to interview someone who knows your child well. Make sure to ask follow-up questions to help you understand the person's perspective.

1. What do you think are the child's strong points (talents, interests)?

2. What specific behaviors concern you?

3. Under what circumstances are these behaviors most likely?
   - With whom:

   - What activities:

   - Where:

   - When:

4. Under what circumstances are these behaviors least likely?
   - With whom:

   - What activities:

   - Where:

   - When:

5. What does it seem to you that the child is getting or avoiding through these behaviors?

6. Can you think of anything else that might be influencing the child's behavior?

Interview Form

Use the following questions to interview someone who knows your child well. Make sure to ask follow-up questions to help you understand the person's perspective.

1. What do you think are the child's strong points (talents, interests)?

2. What specific behaviors concern you?

3. Under what circumstances are these behaviors most likely?
   - With whom:

   - What activities:

   - Where:

   - When:

4. Under what circumstances are these behaviors least likely?
   - With whom:

   - What activities:

   - Where:

   - When:

5. What does it seem to you that the child is getting or avoiding through these behaviors?

6. Can you think of anything else that might be influencing the child's behavior?

Scatterplot

Child: _____   Behavior: _____

Dates: _____ through _____

Record the times of day (and/or activities) in which the behavior might occur. Write in the dates for the recording period in the first row. When the behavior occurs, shade in the corresponding box.

Time	Activity	Dates									

Source: Adapted from Touchette, P. E., MacDonald, R. F., & Langer, S. N. (1985). A scatterplot for identifying stimulus control of problem behavior. *Journal of Applied Behavior Analysis, 18,* 343–351.

Scatterplot

Child: _____   Behavior: _____

Dates: _____ through _____

Record the times of day (and/or activities) in which the behavior might occur. Write in the dates for the recording period in the first row. When the behavior occurs, shade in the corresponding box.

		Dates										
Time	**Activity**											

Source: Adapted from Touchette, P. E., MacDonald, R. F., & Langer, S. N. (1985). A scatterplot for identifying stimulus control of problem behavior. *Journal of Applied Behavior Analysis, 18,* 343–351.

Pattern Analysis Worksheet

Behavior(s) of concern (list all behaviors that reliably occur together): _____

_____

_____

Circumstances	Consequences
My child's problem behavior *usually or often* occurs in the following circumstances:	My child's problem behavior *usually or often* results in the following consequences:
When:	My child gets:
Where:	
With whom:	My child avoids:
What activities:	
My child's problem behavior *rarely or infrequently* occurs in the following circumstances:	My child's positive behavior *usually or often* results in the following consequences:
When:	My child gets:
Where:	
With whom:	My child avoids:
What activities:	

Summary Statement:
Write a sentence or short paragraph to describe the patterns in your child's behavior.

Pattern Analysis Worksheet

Behavior(s) of concern (list all behaviors that reliably occur together): _____

Circumstances	Consequences
My child's problem behavior *usually or often* occurs in the following circumstances:	My child's problem behavior *usually or often* results in the following consequences:
When:	My child gets:
Where:	
With whom:	My child avoids:
What activities:	
My child's problem behavior *rarely or infrequently* occurs in the following circumstances:	My child's positive behavior *usually or often* results in the following consequences:
When:	My child gets:
Where:	
With whom:	My child avoids:
What activities:	

Summary Statement:
Write a sentence or short paragraph to describe the patterns in your child's behavior.

Behavior Log

Record situations in which your child's behavior is difficult, including specifically what your child says and does and what occurs before and after the behavior.

Antecedent (Before Behavior)	Behavior	Consequence (After Behavior)

Behavior Log

Record situations in which your child's behavior is difficult, including specifically what your child says and does and what occurs before and after the behavior.

Antecedent (Before Behavior)	Behavior	Consequence (After Behavior)

Brainstorming Interventions

What circumstances set the stage for my child's behavior?	What is my child currently doing that is of concern?	What outcomes does my child achieve through his or her behavior? Get: Avoid:
PREVENTION:	MANAGEMENT:	REPLACEMENT:
How will I change these things to . . . Avoid difficult situations? Make problem situations better? Add cues to prompt good behavior?	How will I respond to my child's behavior to . . . Reward positive behavior? Not reward problem behavior?	What would I like my child to do instead? How will I teach my child to do this?

Brainstorming Interventions

What circumstances set the stage for my child's behavior?	What is my child currently doing that is of concern?	What outcomes does my child achieve through his or her behavior? Get: Avoid:
PREVENTION:	MANAGEMENT:	REPLACEMENT:
How will I change these things to . . . Avoid difficult situations? Make problem situations better? Add cues to prompt good behavior?	How will I respond to my child's behavior to . . . Reward positive behavior? Not reward problem behavior?	What would I like my child to do instead? How will I teach my child to do this?

Teaching Plan

Develop a plan for teaching a replacement skill to your child.

1. What exactly do you want your child to say or do (steps/components)?

2. Where, when, and with whom (under what circumstances) do you want your child to use this skill?

3. How will you arrange the environment or provide reminders to prompt your child to use this skill?

4. What prompting methods (e.g., describing, showing, gestures, physical guidance) will you use to help your child use the skill?

5. How will you reward your child for using the skill (or making progress in the right direction) and respond to errors when they occur?

6. How will you gradually reduce your assistance and reinforcement over time (to transfer control to your child)?

Teaching Plan

Develop a plan for teaching a replacement skill to your child.

1. What exactly do you want your child to say or do (steps/components)?

2. Where, when, and with whom (under what circumstances) do you want your child to use this skill?

3. How will you arrange the environment or provide reminders to prompt your child to use this skill?

4. What prompting methods (e.g., describing, showing, gestures, physical guidance) will you use to help your child use the skill?

5. How will you reward your child for using the skill (or making progress in the right direction) and respond to errors when they occur?

6. How will you gradually reduce your assistance and reinforcement over time (to transfer control to your child)?

Behavior Support Plan: Part 1

Child's Name:	Date:

Team Members: Who is involved in the process?

Intervention Settings: Where will the plan be used?

Description of Problem Behavior: What does the child say or do?	**Baseline Estimate:** How often? How long?

Broad Goals: How would you like life to improve for your child and family?

Summary Statements: Describe circumstances, behavior, and consequences (get/avoid).

Behavior Support Plan: Part 2

Intervention Components: What strategies will be used (based on the summary statements)?		
Prevention: What changes will be made to avoid problems, make difficult situations better, or prompt good behavior?	**Management:** How will you respond to reward positive behavior and not problem behavior?	**Replacement:** What skills will be taught to replace the problem behavior?

Crisis Management:

Is a plan needed to ensure the safety of your child, other people, and the surroundings? __yes__no

If so, describe strategies:

Other Support: What else can improve life for your child and your family?

Behavior Support Plan: Part 3

Action Plan Steps		
Steps to be taken:	Person responsible:	Time to be completed by:

Monitoring:

How often will the plan be monitored? __ daily __ weekly __ monthly __ other:

How will implementation and outcomes be evaluated?

Monitoring methods (e.g., forms):

Monitoring Form

Our child's behaviors are now happening:

	Never	A few times	Almost every day	More than once per day	Many times per day	Almost every hour	Many times per hour
Problem Behavior							
New Skills							

What other positive or negative changes have occurred for our child and family (e.g., can we go more places or do more things)? _____

_____

_____

_____

_____

Are the strategies included in our behavior plan being used consistently?	Yes	No
Are the strategies included in our behavior plan effective for our child?	Yes	No
Are the strategies included in our behavior plan right for our family?	Yes	No

If the answer is no to any of the previous questions, what kinds of changes do we need to make for the behavior plan to be more effective? _____

_____

_____

_____

_____

CPSIA information can be obtained at www.ICGtesting.com
Printed in the USA
LVOW10s2148040215

425728LV00019B/71/P